THE WORLD OBSERVED / THE WORLD CONCEIVED

THE WORLD **OBSERVED**/THE WORLD **CONCEIVED**

HANS RADDER

UNIVERSITY OF PITTSBURGH PRESS

Published by the University of Pittsburgh Press,
Pittsburgh, Pa., 15260

Library of Congress Cataloging-in-Publication Data
Radder, Hans.
  The world observed, the world conceived / Hans Radder.
      p. cm.
  Includes bibliographical references (p.   ) and index.
  ISBN 0-8229-4284-4 (cloth : alk. paper)
  1. Science—Philosophy. I. Title.
  Q175.R23 2006
  501—dc22
                                        2006008877

For Sally, the *conditio sine qua non*

CONTENTS

This book has a long history. Some of its basic ideas, in particular the distinction between different types of experimental reproducibility and the relation between replicability and abstraction, date back to the late 1980s and early 1990s. In the academic year 1996–1997, I was a fellow at NIAS, the Netherlands Institute for Advanced Study in the Humanities and Social Sciences in Wassenaar. This enabled me to start serious work on the book, which resulted primarily in early versions of the chapters collected in part 1. During the following years, I developed the theory of extensible concepts, abstraction, and nonlocal meaning presented in part 2. This required a study of some areas of philosophy—in particular philosophy of language and ontology—that were relatively unfamiliar to me. The result is a book clearly of a broader scope than the philosophy of science and technology, the field in which I have primarily worked thus far.

As partial results of this research, I published some articles that then provided material for several chapters of this book. Chapter 3 is a revised and expanded version of the first part of my 1999 paper Conceptual and connectionist analyses of observation: A critical evaluation, *Studies in History and Philosophy of Science* 30:455–77; chapter 5 is adapted from the second part of this paper. I thank Elsevier Science, Oxford, UK, for their permission to use this material. Chapters 8–11 build on, but also substantially extend, the discussion in the 2002 article How concepts both structure the world and abstract from it, *Review of Metaphysics* 55:581–613. Chapter 16 appeared in 2004 in more or less its present form as Exploiting abstract possibilities: A critique of the concept and practice of product patenting, *Journal of Agricultural and Environmental Ethics* 17:275–91. I thank Kluwer Academic Publishers, Dordrecht, Netherlands, for their consent to reprint this article. Further permissions for reprinting material were granted by the following publishers: MIT Press, Cambridge, MA (figure

5.1); the Regents of the University of California, Berkeley (figure 6.1); Uitgeverij Boom, Amsterdam (figures 8.1 and 8.2).

While working on the book, I have been encouraged by support and feedback from many people. It is a pleasure to acknowledge their helpfulness in this preface. My sabbatical at NIAS was very stimulating, as were discussions with the other fellows, in particular Stan Judicky, Theo Kuipers, and Marinus van IJzendoorn. Over the years, the meetings of our research group, Knowledge, Normativity and Practice (in the Faculty of Philosophy of the Vrije Universiteit Amsterdam), have always been pleasant and fruitful, and the feedback on drafts of my papers and chapters has always been valuable. Hence, my sincere thanks to Bram Bos Jr., Jaap de Vust, Willem Drees, Kai Eigner, Peter Kirschenmann, Sabina Leonelli, Huib Looren de Jong, Arthur Petersen, Henk de Regt, Frits Schipper, Nikki Smaniotto, Sytse Strijbos, and Han van Diest.

In addition, various colleagues have read and responded to separate chapters or larger parts of the manuscript. I am particularly indebted to Jane Colling, Francesco Guala, Patrick Heelan, Theo Meyering, Menno Rol, Angela Roothaan, Daniel Rothbart, Joseph Rouse, Seth Shulman, Henk van den Belt, Maria van der Schaar, Rasmus Winther, and Sally Wyatt. Further thanks go to the many audiences to which I presented versions of the papers and chapters and to the anonymous reviewers of the University of Pittsburgh Press for their constructive criticisms and suggestions.

I also thank Jane Colling for her accurate and perceptive correction of the English of the final manuscript. Further thanks should go to Kendra Boileau Stokes, Trish Weisman, and others at the University of Pittsburgh Press for their pleasant and professional cooperation in producing this book.

To a certain extent, this book represents a new stage of my philosophical development, corresponding to a new phase of my life. By dedicating the book to Sally, I wish to express my deep gratitude to her. In addition to being a thoughtful and witty partner in many discussions on topics of common interest and being a generous adviser in my struggles with the English language, she is the *conditio sine qua non* of this book.

THE WORLD OBSERVED/THE WORLD CONCEIVED

OBSERVATION AND CONCEPTUAL INTERPRETATION

Most people will agree that observation and conceptual interpretation constitute two major ways through which human beings engage the world. Questions about the character of observation and the nature of concepts, however, have received far fewer unanimous answers. The same applies to claims about the interaction and possible interdependence of observation and conceptual interpretation. In particular, the claims that observation presupposes conceptual interpretation and that concepts can be abstracted from observations have been the subject of fierce philosophical debates.

In this book, I take a fresh look at the nature and role of observation and conceptual interpretation. My approach can be characterized by two general features. First, the slash in the title of the book suggests that observation and conceptual interpretation are not separate issues, but should be seen as interconnected. Indeed, the two principal claims of this book are that materially realized observational processes are always conceptually interpreted and that the meaning of concepts depends on the way they structure observational processes and abstract from them. Of course, the view that observation and interpretation are interconnected has been advocated by quite a few philosophers. I think, however, that the specific articulation of this view, as summarized in its two main claims, may make a useful, novel contribution to the philosophical debate on the subject.

The second general characteristic of the book is its attempt to provide an integrated account of scientific and ordinary life observations and concepts. Hence the book discusses and assesses views from both philosophy of science and other branches of philosophy. There is a certain bias toward philosophy of science, though. This bias is reflected in two ways. First, in line with many contemporary approaches in philosophy of science, the theoretical-philosophical arguments employ results from a variety of studies of concrete observational and conceptual practices. Thus the main claims about the use and meaning of concepts emerge from a discussion of a specific experiment about the development of novel concepts. Such an approach contrasts with philosophical accounts that are supported only by fictitious examples or by unreflectively used illustrations from everyday life. Second, the discussion of both observation and concept formation exploits certain analogies between scientific practice and ordinary life. Several insights from the philosophy of scientific experimentation, in particular concerning the use of instruments and the replicability of experimental results, prove to be fruitful in analyzing human observation and conceptual interpretation more generally. Thus the general analysis of the meaning of concepts draws on an important analogy between the replicability of experimental results and the extensibility of concepts.

Quite a few philosophers who address the problem of observation and conceptual interpretation narrow it down to an exclusively epistemological problem. From this perspective, the main issues are said to be, first, whether observational beliefs of individual human beings may provide us with justified knowledge about an independent world or whether this knowledge is always relative to particular and contingent conceptual frameworks, and second, whether the epistemic value of (direct) observation is superior to the value of (theoretical) conceptualization, as empiricists claim, or the other way round, as rationalists assume.

Although these issues of relativism, empiricism, and rationalism come up occasionally, they are not central to this book. Instead, the focus is on the nature of observation itself and, more particularly, on the conditions of the possibility of human observation. In exclusively epistemological debates this subject is too often taken for granted or inadequately conceptualized. As to concepts, the focus is on the ontological questions of the role of concepts in abstracting from particular observations and the status of concepts as abstract entities. As is demonstrated by the philosophy of language, such questions can be fruitfully discussed without first solving the epistemological problem of relativism, empiricism, or rationalism.

The two major parts of this book address the relationship between observation and conceptual interpretation, but they focus on different aspects of this relationship. Part 2 proposes a novel account of how concepts abstract from particular observations and what this implies for the meaning of these concepts. For this purpose, we first need to develop an appropriate understanding of the notion of observation. This is the primary aim of part 1. It explains this notion as the material realization and conceptual interpretation of observational processes. The principal philosophical thesis of the book may then be concisely phrased as follows. While making observations essentially depends on local material realizations and specific conceptual interpretations, the meaning of the concepts that may be abstracted from these observations is nonetheless nonlocal and open-ended. Put differently and even more concisely: through our concepts we transcend the world as we see it.

While the two parts constitute the main body of the book, the epilogue provides some general reflections on its principal results and on the methods by which these results have been achieved. It relates the proposed notion of observation to wider views of human experience, and it briefly reflects on the position of the book with respect to the metaphilosophical issues of naturalism and critique.

The Material Realization and Conceptual Interpretation of Observational Processes

Observation, whether scientific or ordinary, plays a significant role in many philosophical views. In such views, however, the processes by which observations are made and the conditions that make observations meaningful are often taken for granted or deemed evident. Moreover, in those cases where observation is taken up as a topic of serious research, the resulting analyses and interpretations are diverse and none of them is fully satisfactory.

Thus there is every reason for taking a closer look at the issue of observation. In chapter 7, I provide a philosophical account of observation in terms of the notions of the material realization and conceptual interpretation of observational processes. This account emerges from a critical analysis of several alternative views of the notion of observation (and similar notions, such as experience and perception; in chapters 2–6, I follow these views in their usage of the closely related notions of observation, experience, and perception as being more or less interchangeable). Thus chapters 2–6 discuss and evaluate the accounts of observation given by a number of prominent philosophers of science: Bas van Fraassen, Norwood Hanson, Peter Kosso, Paul Churchland, and Patrick Heelan. Like these authors, I focus on visual observation; the role of the other senses is discussed only occasionally. Furthermore, most of these accounts are embedded in wider views of what it is to observe (or to perceive or experience) something. Accordingly, they do not involve a sharp contrast between ordinary and scientific observation, which is also the position that I take in this book. Chapters 2–6 are ordered according to the (increasing) measure of agreement between the account of observation of the philosopher under discussion and the account of observation proposed in chapter 7.

Chapter 2 starts with a brief discussion of the remarkable lack of philosophical interest in (visual) experience in some empiricist philosophies of science. By way of example, Van Fraassen's views on observation and observability are discussed in some detail. From my perspective, a major problem of empiricist views is the striking contrast between the great significance ascribed to observation, on the one hand, and the absence of a substantive and convincing account of observation, on the other.

The third chapter addresses Hanson's conceptual analysis of observation and, in particular, the debate on the theory ladenness of observation. The claim that observation is theory laden is also part of Kosso's more naturalistic interaction-information theory of scientific observability and observation, which is discussed in chapter 4. The fifth chapter deals with the claims, made by some philosophers of cognitive science (especially Churchland), that connectionism offers an adequate account of observation and that it supports the idea that all observation is theory laden. In these chapters, I argue that the doctrine of theory ladenness can be maintained if it is reformulated as the claim that all observation is conceptually interpreted. Other aspects of the views of Hanson, Kosso, and Churchland, however, are shown to be rather questionable. This applies, in particular, to their complete neglect of the role of human action in making observations.

In phenomenological and hermeneutical philosophy, perception has been a traditional focus of reflection. More recently, some philosophers have applied phenomenological and hermeneutical analyses to scientific observation. In chapter 6, I describe one of these approaches—that proposed by Heelan. In its general outline, this approach puts forward a mostly adequate account of the role of both conceptual interpretation and human action in ordinary and scientific observation. A problem, however, is that Heelan's use of the general notions of interpretation and action in his discussion of more specific subjects is not always satisfactory. This holds, in particular, for his theory of hyperbolic vision.

Chapter 7 employs the results of the preceding chapters in arguing for an account of observation as the material realization and conceptual interpretation of observational processes. The central elements of this account are the notions of an observational process and its material realization and conceptual interpretation. These notions, which arise out of the more specific analyses in chapters 2–6, are explained in a more systematic fashion here. Furthermore, three basic arguments for the claim that all observation requires conceptual interpretation are put forward, and some counterarguments to this claim are discussed and refuted. In addition, the chapter explores an analogy between human observers and scientific instruments. It argues that a human observer may be seen as a self-interpreting observational instrument, which has been brought about in the course of a material and sociocultural evolution and which actively engages the world in attempts at materially realizing and conceptually interpreting observational processes. The chapter concludes with a summarizing account of what it means for an individual observer to observe a particular object or fact.

How Concepts Both Structure the World and Abstract from It

The second part of the book revisits the relationship between (materially realized) observational processes and their conceptual interpretations, but it examines this relationship from a different perspective. The focus is on the meaning of the concepts that are, or may be, employed in interpreting the results of (materially realized) observational processes. More particularly, I discuss the relationship between concepts and the world, where the latter has to be understood as the phenomenal world or the world "as we see it."

In the history of philosophy, two opposing views about the relationship between concepts and the world can be found. One view—deriving from Immanuel Kant and endorsed by Karl Popper, among many others—claims that in forming and using concepts we structure the world. Concepts produce or increase order. Hence the world, in so far as it is knowable by human beings, is necessarily a conceptually structured world. The second, still older view—represented by the (later) Aristotelian tradition and by John Locke, for example—holds that concepts are formed by abstracting from the particularities of the world. By leaving out the spatiotemporality and the accidental or irrelevant features of particular entities, we abstract a concept as a general representative of a (natural) kind.

The principal claim of part 2 of this book is that concepts both structure the world and abstract from it. At first sight, the two parts of this statement appear to be incompatible. I argue, however, not only that they are compatible but that both are necessary to obtain a plausible account of the relationship between concepts and the world. The focus of part 2 is on the problem of abstraction, while the claim that concepts structure the world is dealt with more briefly. I introduce, develop, and vindicate a new account of abstraction that differs from the so-called classical doctrine of abstraction. Central to this account is the idea of the extensibility of concepts to (completely) novel observational processes. The ontological implications of this account are discussed in detail. An important conclusion is that extensible concepts possess a nonlocal meaning.

Chapters 8–11 present the basic ideas about the relationship between concepts and the world. The starting point (chapter 8) is a rendering of Herman Koningsveld's views of the formation and nature of concepts. It involves, in particular, a discussion of an elementary but instructive experiment by which Koningsveld illustrates his view that concepts structure the world. The next chapter proposes a potential replication of this experiment by means of a new observational process. The analysis of Koningsveld's experiment and its suggested replication leads to the introduction of the notions of extensible concepts and their nonlocal meanings. With the help of these notions, I argue that concepts do not just structure the world but also abstract from it. Chapter 10 explains this idea of abstraction in detail and investigates its applicability to the ontological categories of extensible concepts and their referents, the "nonlocals." Among other things, it results in a concise definition of the notion of extensible concepts. Chapter 11 discusses some of the wider philosophical implications of the theory of extensible concepts, abstraction, and nonlocals.

The aim of the next four chapters is to position this theory more precisely with respect to a number of alternative accounts of the issues under discussion. These chapters provide an analysis and evaluation of four alternative views on the nature and function of (scientific and ordinary) concepts and abstraction. Chapter 12 assesses John Haugeland's artificial intelligence account of the related notions of abstraction, formalization, and digitization. Chapter 13 addresses Nancy Cartwright's views on the role of Aristotelian abstraction in scientific theorizing. Bruno Latour's notion of translation and his account of the role of abstract laws and theories are examined in chapter 14. Chapter 15 deals with the theory of meaning finitism, which is advocated by sociologists of scientific knowledge Barry Barnes and David Bloor, among others. Although all four alternatives have their merits, their views of the nature and function of concepts and abstraction are shown to be deficient as compared to the theory of abstraction and nonlocal meaning proposed in this book.

The last chapter of part 2 offers a critique of the concept and practice of a specific kind of patenting, which is called product patenting. The timeliness of this critique derives from the many recent cases of the product patenting of genes. My main point is that what is being patented in this kind of patent is abstract or conceptual possibilities rather than concrete technological inventions. This specific normative critique of the concept and practice of product patenting is shown to follow smoothly from the theoretical-philosophical account of extensible concepts and abstraction.

2

THE ABSENCE OF EXPERIENCE IN EMPIRICISM

If one would like to learn something about experience, one would expect the empiricist tradition to be a rich source of information. This natural expectation does not prove to be generally warranted, though. For instance, if one turns to postwar empiricism in the philosophy of science, one finds a remarkable lack of interest in systematically studying scientific observation. Moreover, the claims that are being made about observation turn out to be inadequate.

It is well-known that, at least by the 1950s and 1960s, the radical empiricism of the early logical positivists had been transformed and weakened. Yet, empiricism remained a basic doctrine within the then-received views in the philosophy of science. Thus Wolfgang Stegmüller (1970, 181–82) still endorses the strong verificationist claim that the truth value of synthetic propositions should be established exclusively on the basis of empirical procedures. The nature of these basic procedures, however, is not investigated at all. For one thing, the index of his voluminous book *Theorie und Erfahrung* does not even contain the item *Erfahrung* (experience) and obviously not for the reason that this notion is discussed passim. According to Stegmüller, a theory of observation might be devised, but it would nonetheless be irrelevant to the fundamental philosophical task of explicating the structure and empirical significance of the language of science. After the linguistic turn, it is the language of science that is taken to be the central topic of philosophical inquiry. The primary subject is not observation itself, but observational statements and, more precisely, the relationship between observational and nonobservational or theoretical statements. Hence, the main philosophical problems are those that arise from the nonobservational nature of theoretical terms.

In a similar vein, in a chapter on "Theories and Nonobservables," Rudolf Carnap briefly discusses the rather different uses of the term "observable" among philosophers and physicists. "A philosopher would not consider a temperature of, perhaps, 80 degrees centigrade, or a weight of 93 1/2 pounds, an observable because there is no direct sensory perception of such magnitudes. To a physicist, both are observables because they can be measured in an extremely simple way" (1966, 225). Carnap concludes that there is no question of who is right and who is wrong. It is a matter of linguistic usage only, since no sharp dividing line exists between the observable and the nonobservable. Apparently, the issue is taken to be philosophically inconsequential. Thus Carnap defines empirical laws as laws containing terms that are either directly observable or relatively simply measurable.[1]

In view of the entire development of logical empiricism, this pragmatic stance may be understandable enough. Yet it leads to serious problems when it is confronted with the verificationist doctrine concerning the truth value of propositions. The critical question that should be (but has not been) faced is this: if the nature of observational processes is irrelevant to the empirical significance of scientific knowledge claims and if the (non)observability of entities is a matter of terminology, what philosophical reason remains for the exclusive epistemological privilege of experience? For instance, on these premises it is no longer obvious that "the observations we make in everyday life as well as the more systematic observations of science *reveal* certain repetitions or *regularities in the world*" (Carnap 1966, 3, emphasis added).

Since the 1980s Bas van Fraassen has developed an empiricist interpretation of science that deviates from the earlier views in some important respects. What remains, though, is the absence of a substantial and adequate account of experience and observation.[2] Again, the focus is on the contrast between observability and nonobservability. As in the case of his predecessors, the real issue for Van Fraassen is theories and the problem of their epistemic and semantic status. Hence, the basic notion of his philosophical account of science is the notion of the empirical adequacy of scientific theories. Yet by comparison with Carnap, Van Fraassen's views are more principled. He takes observation to be an unaided act of visual perception, a seeing with the naked eye. Hence, in his account observation is sharply opposed to instrumentally mediated detection (Van Fraassen 1980, 13–19, 56–59).

Apart from this, there are some further contrasts with traditional empiricist views. First, Van Fraassen makes a distinction between observing something and observing-that something is the case. Thus, he says, the fact that "someone observed the tennis ball" does not necessarily imply that "this person observed-that it was a tennis ball." Van Fraassen agrees with many contemporary philosophers that "observing-that p" is "theory laden": it presupposes a certain conceptual, linguistic, or theoretical interpretation of p. Yet one of the points of his position is his claim that the observability of something is an empirical, theory-independent fact. Next, he admits that being observable—that is to say, being perceivable with the naked eye—is a vague predicate in the sense that a border zone exists where it is hard to say whether the entities in question are observable or not. However, he thinks that the existence of borderline cases does not constitute a real problem, because clear examples and counterexamples of observable entities and properties are easy to offer. Finally, Van Fraassen insists that the location of the border, or border zone, between what is and what is not observable for human beings is a matter to be settled by empirical science and not by philosophical fiat. "The human organism is, from the point of view of physics, a certain kind of measuring apparatus. As such it has certain inherent limitations—which will be described in detail in the final physics and biology. It is these limitations to which the 'able' in 'observable' refers—our limitations *qua* human beings" (Van Fraassen 1980, 17). These claims introduce a naturalist element into Van Fraassen's empiricist philosophy, even if he also argues against the Quinean project of a fully naturalized empiricist epistemology (see Van Fraassen 1995).

Problems of the Constructive Empiricist Approach to Observation
and Observability

Van Fraassen has developed a comprehensive philosophical interpretation of science, called constructive empiricism, of which his views on observation and observability form merely a small, albeit a crucial, part.[3] Given the aim of this book, my focus is on the constructive empiricist notion of experience, while the other aspects of Van Fraassen's philosophical interpretation of science are largely ignored here. In particular, this applies to the implications of my evaluation of Van Fraassen's views of observation and observability for the general theory of constructive empiricism.

I begin with a comment on the above quotation. In contrast to Van Fraassen, I do not think that referring to "the final physics and biology" is helpful for an understanding of the notions of observability and observation. First, as philosophers we cannot wait that long. If we want to discuss and assess the role of experience in present-day science and ordinary life, we need an adequate account of the notions of observability and observation.[4] Second, it is highly speculative and questionable whether there will ever be a final physics and biology. And third, as we will see in detail in the chapters that follow, there is much more to observability and observation than just physics and biology.

A further problem relates to the distinction between observing and observing-that. The claim is that "observing something" is not conceptually interpreted or theory laden, even if "observing-that something is the case" always is. Van Fraassen concludes from this claim that the observability of an entity or property is not dependent on the concepts or theories which the observer, explicitly or implicitly, endorses.[5] At first sight, this conclusion might seem to run counter to the naturalistic requirement that only science (including scientific theories) can tell us what human beings can or cannot observe. This problem can be resolved, though, by realizing that we have to distinguish between, on the one hand, the empirical fact that certain things are observable for human beings and, on the other, the issue of how science might account for this fact (see Van Fraassen 1980, 57–58).

Van Fraassen supports the claim that observing something is not conceptually interpreted or theory laden with the help of the example of the tennis ball. His interpretation of this example is questionable, though. The problem is that observers may fail to observe-that the object in question is a tennis ball because they observe-that it is a baseball or perhaps because they merely observe-that it is an unidentified flying object. In this case, the tennis ball example merely exemplifies different instances of observing-that rather than the distinction between theory- or concept-independent observing and theory-laden or conceptually interpreted observing-that. In the following chapters, especially chapters 3 and 7, I develop this point and argue for the view that observing something always involves conceptual interpretation.

A typical feature of Van Fraassen's empiricism is his uncompromising view that only observation with the naked eye carries epistemic weight. He realizes that this makes epistemological conclusions dependent on the contingent condition of human sense organs. He does not count this as an objection, though, since it is precisely what one should expect in an antimetaphysical, empiricist account of human observation. If we happened to have electron microscope eyes, an empiricist would of course reach different conclusions as to which claims are epistemologically justified.

Yet, if we leave science fiction aside and turn to actual practice, there is a problem here. Consider all those scientific observers who wear contact lenses. A contact lens is an instrument designed to improve human eyesight. From a technological point of view it is as sophisticated and high tech as a microscope, and the theoretical explanation of how a contact works employs the same optical principles as are used in the case of the microscope.

Van Fraassen (1980, 18) claims that, at present, our epistemic community coincides with the human race. His empiricist stance, however, implies that scientists who wear contact lenses are, in a certain respect, inferior members of this epistemic community. Their observations carry epistemic weight only because and in so far as they can be confirmed through direct perceptions by scientists with "normal" eyesight. A plausible justification of this epistemological discrimination, however, is lacking. The same point can be made even more convincingly by imagining that in, say, fifty years all scientists will wear contact lenses. Surely, this is a hypothetical situation but it is certainly not impossible or far-fetched. According to Van Fraassen, however, this state of affairs would necessarily imply the end of science as we know it. Again, there is the question of an adequate reason for this epistemological judgment, given that the wearing of contact lenses does not affect the actual practice of science in any significant way.

The older empiricists had at least an answer, albeit an untenable one, to these problems. They assumed that unmediated observation could provide an indubitable and theory-independent foundation for scientific knowledge. Van Fraassen, in contrast, agrees that all observational claims—all observing-that something is the case—are theory relative, and hence he must deny a foundational role for observation. In addition, scientific accounts of the operation of eye lenses and contact lenses point out their functional equivalence. Thus both theory ladenness and a naturalistic account of observational processes make it difficult, if not impossible, to find any good reason for upholding Van Fraassen's principled distinction between unaided and contact lens observation. Hence, in developing my own account of observation, I draw on the analogy, rather than on the contrast, between unaided human observation and instrumental detection.

Finally, Van Fraassen's account suffers from the following problem. His primary notion is observability rather than observation. However, the two notions are related. Thus, as a "rough guide" to the notion of observability, Van Fraassen explains that "X is observable if there are circumstances which are such that, if X is present to us under those circumstances, then we observe it" (Van Fraassen 1980, 16).

Unfortunately, he does not go on to provide an informed account of the specific circumstances that enable the actual observation of X. In a more recent publication, he at least mentions some of these circumstances by pointing out that observational reports are adjusted "for wear and tear, noise and interference, and so forth, in the usual scientific way"; in addition, he states that experience only counts if it is "relevant," and he claims that telepathic experiences, even if they are confirmed through normal observations, are not a relevant source of scientific data (see Van Fraassen 1995, 73–76). Again, however, these points remain undeveloped since they are merely put forward as a means to a quite different philosophical end, namely, as premises in an argument against the feasibility of a fully naturalized, empiricist philosophy.

The same problem can be phrased somewhat differently as follows. In his latest book, Van Fraassen provides a detailed and quite favorable discussion of Paul Feyerabend's views on the theory ladenness of observation and on the incommensurability of theories (Van Fraassen 2002, 111–52). Feyerabend's criticism, however, was also directed at a "crude empiricism" that encourages "the uncritical collection and preservation of facts" and the "quite extraordinary credulity extended to the reports of eyewitnesses" (1965, 156; on this point, see also Nagel 2000). Remarkably enough, Van Fraassen does not address this part of Feyerabend's arguments at all. For this reason, he is unable to systematically discuss and answer the question of which kinds of observational circumstances make our experiences cognitively or epistemically relevant.[6]

Recently, Van Fraassen's views have been examined in detail by several authors. In large part, these studies address issues (for instance, regarding the debate between constructive empiricism and scientific realism) that are clearly distinct from the subject of the present discussion. But in so far as they engage Van Fraassen's views of observation and observability, they are not very helpful in tackling the problems put forward here.

At one extreme, Stathis Psillos inflates the notion of observability by claiming that viruses may be observed by human beings who have been shrunken to the size of these entities (1999, 190–91). Referring to Van Fraassen's own endorsement of the observability of the moons of Jupiter, he writes, "If we call the satellites of Saturn 'observable' because we can imagine (that is, because it is consistent with the laws of nature to imagine) technological innovations which, although still unavailable, can make us directly observe the satellites, then we should allow viruses to be *observable*" (190). However, while the laws of nature do allow for space travel to Saturn, scaling down human beings to the size of a virus and, in particular, assuming that such creatures would still possess appropriate sense organs, really is a fiction. On this point, I agree with Van Fraassen that a plausible account of human observation and observability should not depend on implausible science fiction stories.

At the other extreme Fred Muller, writing in the spirit of Van Fraassen, claims that the scientific problem of what is observable and what is not was solved some time ago.

The empirical inquiries into the observability of objects have been pursued actively in the 1950s and 1960s and came to an end (or a provisional end) some time ago. Enough results had apparently been gathered. (All currently flourishing research into the human eye is research about the cognitive capabilities of the visual system as a whole and about where precisely in the brain things happen that are relevant for seeing, and where and how the "visual information is processed." Which objects are visible under which circumstances—the only relevant question for us—is now a depleted area of research). (2005, 86–87)

Unfortunately, this is too good to be true. For one thing, just recently new developments have been taking place in the area of visual science. A striking example is the article by J. Kevin O'Regan and Alva Noë, entitled "A sensorimotor account of vision and visual consciousness" (2001a). This article is followed by no less than forty-one different open peer commentaries, which are partly critical and partly supportive. Apparently, the visual scientists themselves see their field as far from "depleted." Furthermore, this literature is really relevant to the question of "which objects are visible under which circumstances," as is apparent from the occurrence of so-called change blindness effects, which I discuss briefly in chapter 7. Finally, and most importantly, O'Regan and Noë advocate a view of seeing as a way of acting, a way of exploring the environment. By taking into account the interaction between the entire human organism and the environment, this view clearly contrasts to the theory suggested by Muller, which is limited to the physics of the object, the light, and the eye.

In conclusion, empiricist philosophers of science have thus far failed to provide a convincing account of experience. In the subsequent chapters I provide a detailed examination of the problems that I put forward here as a criticism of constructive empiricism. Solving these problems is crucial to obtaining an adequate understanding of the nature of scientific and ordinary experience.

3

THE CONCEPTUAL ANALYSIS OF OBSERVATION

A number of nonempiricist philosophers have addressed the issue of the nature and role of (scientific and everyday) experience in more substantial ways. Their views are discussed in this and the next three chapters. Here I focus on the conceptual analysis of observation. This approach is illustrated by Norwood Hanson's sophisticated and still worthwhile account of observation. His most important achievement is the introduction and explication of the idea that observation is theory laden. The idea was introduced in Hanson's *Patterns of Discovery* (1972, first edition 1958). In this book, he also uses the locution theory loaded, apparently without differentiating between the two terms. In the literature the expression theory laden has become entrenched, and I conform to this usage. In contemporary philosophy, the view that observation is theory laden finds both supporters and critics. Hence, any systematic analysis of the notion of observation should address this issue in detail. My analysis concludes that a revised version of the idea of theory ladenness can be upheld but that Hanson's account is nevertheless seriously deficient as a comprehensive view of ordinary and scientific observation.

Building in part on the later work of Ludwig Wittgenstein, Hanson's aim is a philosophical explication of our normal notion of seeing or observing, and his method is that of a conceptual analysis of the way this notion is used in (ordinary or scientific) language and practice. Given this aim and this method, analyses of the physical or physiological process of observation are claimed to be irrelevant. Thus Hanson remarks that seeing is an experience, not a physical state, and that it is people, not their eyes, that see. In support of this he argues that having a certain retinal image is clearly different from making a relevant observation. Drunk, drugged, hypnotized, or distracted people may not see an object in front of them, even if they have a normal retinal image of it (1972, 6).

Since he uses illustrations from ordinary life and from scientific practice indiscriminately, Hanson clearly intends to imply that there is no essential difference between ordinary seeing and scientific observation. The main question, then, is what is implied when we, in ordinary life or in ordinary science, say that we see or observe something? Hanson tackles this question by investigating the conditions under which different people can be said to see (or not to see) the same thing.

To illuminate the notion of seeing the same thing, he examines cases where what we see is controversial, ambiguous, or context dependent (Hanson 1972, 4–19; 1969, chap. 5). Thus he imagines a controversy concerning the question of what Tycho Brahe and Johannes Kepler see at dawn. In an important sense, Hanson claims, they do not see the same thing. Brahe, from a geocentric perspective, sees the sun rise, while Kepler, from the heliocentric point of view, sees the earth turn away. Hence, Hanson concludes that similar visual stimuli may lead to quite different observations. He further substantiates this conclusion by referring to the well-known phenomenon of perceptual ambiguity. Here he shows and discusses some of the many pictures of the duck-rabbit variety, which may be seen alternately in two quite distinct ways. Finally, he stresses that what one observes depends on previous training and on the context in which one is situated. A trained physicist sees an X-ray tube on the laboratory bench, where a layperson merely sees a complex thing composed of glass, metal plates, wires, and the like.

In making these claims, Hanson is well aware of other possible interpretations of the notion of seeing the same thing. Thus he by no means denies that, in a certain sense, Brahe and Kepler do see the same dawn. "We must proceed carefully, for wherever it makes sense to say that two scientists looking at x do not see the same thing, there must always be a prior sense in which they do see the same thing. The issue is, then, 'Which of these senses is most illuminating for the understanding of observational physics?'" (1972, 5).

In arguing against the empiricist view of observation as the foundation of knowledge, Hanson stresses the sense in which seeing the same thing is a

context-relative matter. More precisely, it is the organization and appreciation of what we see that is affected by contextually variable factors.

Which factors are these? In Hanson's analyses, we find a variety of desig-
nations: conceptual organization, language, knowledge, and theory. "Tycho
sees the sun beginning its journey from horizon to horizon. . . . Kepler's visual field, however, has a different conceptual organization" (1972, 23).
"There is a sense . . . in which seeing is a 'theory-laden' undertaking. Observation of x is shaped by prior knowledge of x. Another influence on observation rests in the language or notation used to express what we know, and
without which there would be little we could recognize as knowledge" (19).

In many discussions, starting with Hanson's, these claims are summarized in the slogan that observation is theory laden. In this sense, Kepler's
seeing of the earth turning away at dawn is said to be laden with Cop-
ernicus's heliocentric theory, while Brahe's seeing the sun rise is laden with
the geocentric theory of the solar system.

Finally, Hanson explains the theory ladenness of observation by referring to two important elements of our concept of seeing: seeing-as and seeing-that. Thus Kepler sees what he sees as the (Copernican) sun. More generally, seeing a thing, "is *seeing* it *as* this sort of thing or as that sort of thing;
we do not just *see* indeterminately or in general, as do infants and lunatics.
And seeing a thing as *this* or *that* presupposes a *knowledge* of *this* or *that* sort
of thing" (1969, 107).

Moreover, in the case of seeing-that, an even stronger link exists between
observation on the one hand and concepts, language, knowledge, and theory on the other. An indication of this is the fact that "I see that" should be
followed by a full declarative sentence. "'Seeing that' threads knowledge
into our seeing; it saves us from re-identifying everything that meets our
eye; it allows physicists to observe new data as physicists, and not as cam-
eras. We do not ask 'What's that?' of every passing bicycle. The knowledge is
there in the seeing and not an adjunct of it" (Hanson 1972, 22).

According to Hanson, seeing-as and seeing-that should not be conceived
as being separate parts within a more general psychological process of seeing. Instead, they are logically implied in our concept of seeing. Moreover,

he emphasizes that they must be implied if observation is to have any significance at all for the making of knowledge (1972, 25; 1969, 125). In this
sense, seeing-as and seeing-that constitute inextricable and indispensable
elements of seeing as a cognitively and epistemically significant achievement. Through seeing-as and seeing-that, observation is conceptually organized or shaped by prior knowledge, and influenced by the language or
laden with the theory in which this knowledge may be expressed. In this
sense, Hanson's notion of theory ladenness applies primarily to (our concept of) observation and not just to observation statements or observation
reports.

Theory Ladenness Reconsidered

So much for Hanson's account of (scientific) observation. My evaluation of
this account does not aim at comprehensiveness.[1] On the positive side, a
notable virtue is that Hanson, unlike most of his empiricist predecessors,
does not take the concepts of experience and observation for granted but
thinks them worthy of, and amenable to, systematic philosophical analysis.
An important result of this analysis is that the same visual stimuli may, and
often do, lead to different observations. One may add to this that psychological experiments also show the reverse: distinct visual stimuli may well
result in the same observations. A well-known illustration is provided by
the variety of experiments in which experimental subjects wore glasses that
consistently distorted their normal optical images. In spite of their diver-
gent visual stimuli, after some time of training the subjects tended to see
the world as they previously did.

Thus the relation between stimulus and observation is in principle a
many-to-many relation. What follows is a familiar, albeit a negative, conclusion: because concepts, knowledge, language, and theory play an inter-
mediary role in observation, there is no direct and unique route between
sensory stimuli and observational (let alone theoretical) knowledge claims.
For this reason, observation does not and cannot function as the exclusive
foundation of (scientific) knowledge.

There is, however, an important further conclusion to be drawn, and it goes beyond what Hanson is prepared to endorse. In his description of what Brahe and Kepler see, Hanson admits that there is a prior sense in which they do see the same thing. More generally, he acknowledges that there are genuine cases of what he calls phenomenal seeing (1969, 108–10). For instance, when we are confused or when we do not know what we see, we report our observations in some sort of sense-datum terminology, such as "x has a green tint to it in this light." According to Hanson, such cases occur, but they are untypical, they are not paradigm cases of seeing and certainly not of scientific observation.[2]

I think, however, that this is an unnecessary concession to phenomenalist theories of perception. After all, even these simple observations involve seeing-as or seeing-that. Thus in the example of "x has a green tint to it in this light," we see x as having a green tint and we do acknowledge the fact that the kind of light is a relevant factor in color perception. In the same way as seeing a bear climbing up the other side of a tree (discussed below), seeing a green thing requires a specific organization of our visual field (compare with Koningsveld 1973, 14–37). More generally, as many studies have shown (see Van Brakel 1993), color perception is historically and anthropologically variable. Hence neither color nor anything else can serve as a plausible example of a sense datum.

The notions of seeing-as and seeing-that most clearly show that seeing is always intentional. That is to say, it purports to be about entities that are external to the entities that make up our sensory apparatus. Furthermore, the involvement of seeing-as and seeing-that entails that any act of seeing or observing—which as a matter of fact occurs in a particular, local situation—is always related to something that transcends that situation. In seeing-as there is an implicit relation to what we know about other (similar or dissimilar) situations, and in seeing-that there is an implicit connection to linguistically expressible knowledge claims.

Despite these valuable results, there are also reasons for criticism of Hanson's account of observation. The doctrine of the theory ladenness of observation has been broadly agreed upon by a considerable number of philosophers of science (such as Karl Popper, Thomas Kuhn, Paul Feyerabend, Imre Lakatos, Bas van Fraassen, and Paul Churchland), even if they differ greatly on its exact philosophical interpretation and significance. However, the claim that observation is theory laden has also received substantial criticisms, for example, from Abner Shimony, Ian Hacking, Richard Grandy, and Jerry Fodor. Hence, if we want to support the intuition underlying this claim, we have to face these criticisms.

As I have explained, Hanson actually uses a number of different notions to characterize what observation is laden with. Thus he claims that observation is essentially shaped by concepts, by language, by knowledge, and by theory. It is clear, though, that, taken separately, the meaning of those notions is far from straightforward, while, taken jointly, they can be expected to exhibit substantial differences. Hence it is not surprising that the summary slogan that observation is "theory laden" is too crude to take account of the possible distinctions within and between these different notions. In this vein, several criticisms have been leveled at this slogan.

Thus Grandy (1992, 202–4) argues that we should distinguish between different senses of theory ladenness. According to Grandy, scientific observations (for instance, seeing that the object x is at a distance of 2.10^{13} meters from the observer) may depend on quite different kinds of theories: theories of instruments, theories of measurement scales, data-processing theories, computational theories, theories underlying the conceptual organization, and so on. Furthermore, Hacking (1983, 171–72) points out that not all ladenness is theory ladenness: many assumptions implied in cases of seeing-as or seeing-that (for example, seeing a gash as a wound) are misdescribed when they are called scientific theories. Finally, Shimony (1977, 191–92) criticizes Hanson for leaving unclear the nature, scope, and mode of operation of the conceptual frameworks that organize our visual field. Are there different types of organizing concepts? Are some concepts universally shared or perhaps even innate? Are some of our organizing concepts under conscious control? According to Shimony, Hanson fails to pose and answer such crucial Kantian questions.[3]

Generally speaking, such criticisms are pertinent. Yet it is not too difficult to take them into account in a way that remains congenial to Hanson's position. However, first note that in the 1950s, empiricist foundationalism was far more dominant than it is nowadays. Hence the admittedly careless use of the notion of theory may be understood if we interpret Hanson's claim as first and foremost critical, to wit, directed against empiricist foundationalism. In this context, the vague term "theory" simply stands for all inputs that are not derivable from sensation, that are—as it were—added from elsewhere to the local perceptual situation. In the same spirit, Feyerabend uses a very broad notion of a theory. "In what follows, the term 'theory' will be used in a wide sense, including ordinary beliefs (e.g., the belief in the existence of material objects), myths (e.g., the myth of eternal recurrence), religious beliefs, etc. In short, any sufficiently general point of view concerning matter of fact will be termed a 'theory'" (1965, 219). In contrast, Hacking (1983, 175) defines a theory much more narrowly as "some fairly specific body of speculation or propositions with a definite subject matter."

However this may be, the criticisms of the thesis of theory ladenness can be accommodated if we accept as the core of the argument the claim that all seeing involves seeing-as and hence that all observation essentially requires conceptual interpretation (or organization/structuring). Then the precise nature of these concepts (their linguistic expression, their theoretical character, and their relation to explicit knowledge claims) may be taken to vary in separate cases and hence to be a subject for more specific research. The same applies to the scope of such concepts (local, nonlocal, or universal) and to their mode of operation (conscious or unconscious). Thus Fodor (1984) may well be right in that some of the concepts on which observation depends are universal or that some of them do vary but not as a result of a conscious decision. Yet this by no means justifies his further claim that there is a theory-neutral observation/inference distinction.[4]

In infants, conceptually interpreted observation (or seeing-as) may precede the ability of linguistically expressing and explicitly formulating the knowledge that is assumed in seeing-that. This fact provides another reason for taking seeing-as, and not seeing-that, to be the most basic and the most general form of conceptually interpreted observation. Thus my revision of the theory ladenness thesis can be summarized in the claim that all observations involve seeing-as.

The philosophical notion of seeing-as, which is claimed to be involved in all seeing, cannot be generally identified with our common sense notion of seeing-as. As Norman (1998, 506) rightly concludes, both in ordinary and in scientific language seeing is not synonymous with seeing-as. What is meant by saying that all observations involve seeing-as, however, is that seeing is like seeing-as in that it involves an element of construal, even if it is unlike seeing-as in its implied commitment to the existence and presence of what has been seen (compare with Norman 1998).

Compared with the doctrine of the theory ladenness of observation, the claim that all observation involves seeing-as and hence conceptual interpretation is somewhat less specific, but it is more plausible and still philosophically nontrivial. It warns us not to identify physical or physiological stimuli with observational content. In particular, it contrasts to the views that "only what we think we see is knowledge dependent, whereas what we see is determined by reality" (Derksen 1980, 244) and that "there is a class of beliefs that are typically fixed by sensory/perceptual processes" (Fodor 1984, 24).

Neglect of the Observational Process and the Role of Human Action

There are further—and much more serious—problems in Hanson's account of observation. These problems derive from the fact that Hanson neglects several important aspects of the observational process because his focus is on the result of this process. He discusses primarily the issue of what we see, but his account of the circumstances that enable us to see what we see is ambiguous and significantly incomplete.

First, Hanson's view of the philosophical relevance of physical or physiological accounts of the observational process is ambiguous. On the one hand, at a metaphilosophical level he advocates the method of conceptual analysis. His aim is to explain the presuppositions and implications of our concept of observation. From this perspective, he claims that physics and physiology are irrelevant because seeing is not the same as having a certain retinal image. Now naturalists may well agree with the latter part of this claim, but they do not need to see it as a refutation of naturalism. After all, they may simply reply that the eye covers only a part of the observational system and that a satisfactory account should, of course, be based on an analysis of the full physical and physiological processes. This seems to be the approach taken by Peter Kosso, which I discuss in the next chapter.

On the other hand, at times Hanson does have recourse to factual information about observational processes. Thus he criticizes two-stage accounts of seeing as sensation plus subsequent interpretation on the grounds that seeing is one holistic and immediate act, while interpretation is a process that takes time. More generally, he uses the results of psychological experiments to support his view that the same stimulus does not necessarily entail the same experience. Given his definition of philosophy as conceptual analysis, the precise evidential role of psychological experiments remains unclear, though (compare with Hanson 1972, 179).

In addition to being ambiguous, Hanson's account is also seriously incomplete, because it unjustly neglects the role of human action in realizing observational processes. Examples taken from Hanson himself help explain this. He presents the drawing of figure 3.1 and claims to see "a bear climbing up the other side of a tree" (Hanson 1972, 12–13; 1969, 121–23). And although some people may not at all see a bear in this figure, I assume—for the sake of argument—that this is indeed what we see.

What is implied in this act of seeing, however, is not merely conceptual organization. Apparently, we immediately see that this drawing is an, admittedly rather schematic, two-dimensional representation of a three-dimensional object. This means that the tree represented in this figure has an

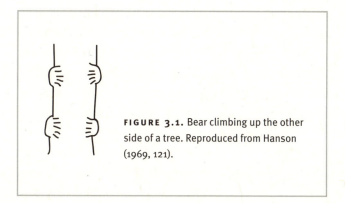

FIGURE 3.1. Bear climbing up the other side of a tree. Reproduced from Hanson (1969, 121).

"other side." On the basis of preceding experiences with a real tree, we know that we could walk around such a tree and have a look at the other side. Combining our seeing of the front side with this imaginary seeing of the back side, we come to see the figure as a bear climbing up the other side of a tree. Thus the circumstances that enable this particular act of seeing-as include the possibility of (preceding) locomotion.

As Willem Drees pointed out (personal communication), there may be an alternative interpretation. It might be that seeing figure 3.1 as a bear climbing up the other side of a tree derives from an earlier experience in which the bear, instead of the observer, happened to turn around the tree. Although this interpretation is possible in this particular case, it does not apply to two-dimensional pictures of fixed three-dimensional objects, such as a hill or a house. Hence, it cannot be taken as generally valid.

A further objection might be that the example is not representative because of the highly schematic nature of figure 3.1. In this vein, Jane Colling suggested (personal communication) that the success of this specific act of seeing-as can be explained with reference to the presence and function of a particular, though widely recognized, cartoon style. Her point is that locomotion has no part to play, since this mental process of seeing-as merely involves inference, namely, an inference from a cartoon part to a cartoon whole.

Replying to this objection also clarifies my critique of Hanson's account of seeing. One of the points of this critique is to highlight the significance of the relation between two-dimensional images (whether schematic or not) and the three-dimensional objects they are supposed to represent. This point is not limited to cartoons but has a much more general significance. Another illustration can be found in Daniel Rothbart's discussion of the role of schematic pictorial images in the design and use of instruments and apparatuses in engineering practice. Rothbart builds on James Gibson's more general account of how we perceive such schematic drawings. "Gibson . . . has demonstrated empirically that surfaces are perceived through the experience of occluding edges. An occluding edge has a double life: it hides some surfaces and exposes others" (Rothbart 2003, 242; see also Gibson 1986).

The phenomenon of occlusion is not limited to schematic drawings, however; it applies just as well to the perception of three-dimensional objects, such as apples or spectrometers. "Occlusion draws upon a history of past perceptions and invites exploration of future possibilities, imagining surfaces from different perspectives. Whether perceiving apples or the metal and wires of a spectrometer, an observer recognizes how attributes would change as a result of movement around corners, under or even through a material body to recover 'hidden' surfaces" (Rothbart 2003, 243). Rothbart goes on to discuss the nature and function of schematic drawings of instruments in engineering practices.

Three points emerge from this account. First, it is clearly the case that perceiving such pictorial images draws on a particular practice and requires particular skills, just like the perception of the cartoonlike bear. Yet the point of the discussion is that it shows what is revealed about three-dimensional objects by means of observing two-dimensional images. Through perceiving a schematic drawing of an absorption spectrometer an engineer learns something about the spectrometer itself, not just about a picture of it. Furthermore, this practice of reading three-dimensional information from two-dimensional clues makes sense only on the basis of the success of preceding experiences of locomotion (and, see below, other forms of action). As Rothbart explains, what may happen under imagined movements can only be perceived on the basis of real movements that have been successfully performed at some time in the past. Finally, and most importantly, whenever we perceive real objects (a real bear, a real apple, or a real spectrometer), we always see those objects from a specific perspective. We never observe an object in its full, three-dimensional sense but only through one or more of its "profiles." For this reason, the claim that observing an object presupposes the possibility of (preceding) action applies not only to the perception of (schematic) two-dimensional images but also to real three-dimensional objects. Thus, generally speaking, seeing-as depends not only on conceptual organization but also on the mobility of the human body.

It is instructive to contrast this account with the one provided by Hanson. He says that seeing figure 3.1 as a bear climbing up the other side of a tree is simply to see that, were the other side depicted, we would see the re-

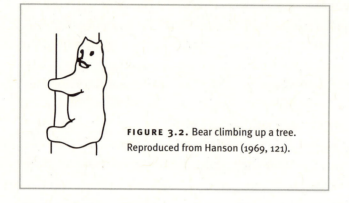

FIGURE 3.2. Bear climbing up a tree.
Reproduced from Hanson (1969, 121).

maining parts of the bear, for instance as in figure 3.2 (Hanson 1969, 121).
I do not deny that this is true. But the point is that a mere juxtaposition of
figure 3.1 and figure 3.2 is not enough to integrate them into the seeing of a
complete bear, through seeing them as front and back, respectively. In other
words, to see figure 3.2 as implied by figure 3.1, we first have to see figure 3.1
as a bear climbing up the other side of a tree, and this presupposes the possibility of locomotion. This may look only slightly different, but the difference is significant. In Hanson's view, the observer's involvement is disembodied and it merely consists of conceptual, linguistic, or theoretical
contributions, whereas the significance of locomotion is neglected.

A similar point has been made by Shimony, who contrasts the sparsity
of the stimuli presented in the psychological experiments discussed by
Hanson to the richness of stimuli under ordinary circumstances. "One
source of richness is the simultaneous involvement of several senses. Another is the array of 'higher order variables of stimulus,' such as spatial and
temporal gradients, which are capable of conveying decisive information.
Finally, in ordinary situations there are usually opportunities for exploration, by motion of the organism as a whole or by movements of the
eyes, hands, and head, for the purpose of bringing small cues into promi-
nence and achieving new perspectives" (1977, 196).[5]

My discussion to this point stresses the significance of the locomotion of
the entire organism. Shimony rightly adds that movements of body parts,
such as eyes, hands, and head, are also crucially important in successfully

realizing observational processes. A further example reinforces the general point. Hanson starts his discussion of the issue of observation as follows. "Consider two microbiologists. They look at a prepared slide; when asked what they see, they may give different answers. One sees in the cell before him a cluster of foreign matter; it is an artefact, a coagulum resulting from inadequate staining techniques. . . . The other biologist identifies the clot as a cell organ, a 'Golgi body'" (Hanson 1972, 4).

What is involved in this case is not only movement of body parts and locomotion, but active human intervention. First note that the microbiologists do not look at a "given" substance but rather at an artificially prepared cell. The observational process includes a stage of active interference with the "observable" object. Furthermore, their controversy over what they see bears on the (in)adequacy of the fixing and staining techniques by which this particular cell has been prepared. Their seeing-that presupposes a certain know-how about what is or what is not an adequate staining technique in cases like these. Hanson, however, does not draw such conclusions. He considers this biological example as being "too complex" and therefore turns to the case of what Kepler and Brahe see at dawn. This move, however, is by no means a harmless simplification, since it results in a one-sided focus on conceptual, linguistic, and theoretical matters. It reinforces the tendency to neglect the role of movements of body parts, (potential and actual) locomotion, and intervention. In sum, in this way the significance of human action is being ignored.

This focus and this neglect fit in well with Hanson's view of knowledge as exclusively linguistic. He delimits knowledge as pertaining to a system of propositions and stresses the significance of intersubjective communication of knowledge through its linguistic expressions. From this point of view, practical know-how and individual skill may influence the direction of research, but in the end they are irrelevant for a philosophical interpretation of knowledge, since they do not affect the content of science (Hanson 1972, 26; 1969, 125–26).

Unfortunately, his own example of the controversy between the two microbiologists appears to belie this view. At issue here is not primarily the direction of microbiological research but rather a fact, to wit, whether there is a Golgi body present or not. Seeing-that there is a Golgi body presupposes that the normal fixing and staining conditions have been skillfully realized in the case in question. Thus the content of science depends on what we observe, while what we observe will be affected by our know-how. As Hacking rightly remarks, "Observation is a skill. Some people are better at it than others. You can often improve this skill by training and practice" (1983, 168). That is to say, the conditions for correctly seeing-as and seeing-that include such practical matters as being sufficiently skilled.

Let me finish this chapter by summing up the main conclusions. First, I endorse the claim that sense perception does not and cannot provide an exclusive foundation of knowledge. Next, I point out that all seeing involves seeing-as and often also seeing-that. Consequently, all seeing is conceptually interpreted. Furthermore, I argue that observation also depends on human action, for example, in the form of movements of body parts, of (potential and actual) locomotion, or of intervention. It is primarily the absence of any reference to human action and, more generally, to the material realization of observational processes, that entails the inadequacy of Hanson's theory of everyday and scientific observation.

THE INTERACTION-INFORMATION THEORY OF

OBSERVABILITY AND OBSERVATION

While Norwood Hanson's approach is limited to a conceptual analysis of what we see, Peter Kosso offers a more comprehensive view by taking into account the observational processes through which we see what we see. In his 1989 book, *Observability and Observation in Physical Science,* he provides a detailed account of a variety of observational processes. As the title of this book indicates, his focus is on physical science. Yet, since he draws heavily on Fred Dretske's (1981) analyses of ordinary perception, his main results may well be more widely applicable than to physical science alone.

The basic point of Kosso's view is that the goal of observation is to acquire information about more or less distant objects x and their properties P by means of an interaction between these object-property pairs and an observer. Hence, the name interaction-information account. Furthermore, he takes the interaction to be of a purely physical kind, in the sense of a process, or chain of processes, to be analyzed with the help of physical theories. Usually, in scientific observations one or more apparatuses are inserted between the objects to be observed and the final human observer. In these terms, an observation is defined as follows. "The ordered pair <object x, property P> is observed to the extent that there is an interaction (or a chain of interactions) between x and an observing apparatus such that the information 'that x is P' is conveyed to a human scientist" (Kosso 1989, 32). Thus Kosso advocates a naturalistic and empirical approach to the issues of observability and observation. The task is to describe and analyze the ways in which, according to our physical theories, information can be or is being acquired in concrete cases of observational interactions in science. The proper question is not, is x (un)observable? but rather, in what way is x (un)observable in scientific practice?

In this spirit, Kosso (1989, chap. 3) introduces a useful distinction between three different cases of observability. First, there are things that are unobservable in principle. In this case, the relevant theories of the observational process imply that no interaction at all is possible between these things and any apparatus or human observer. The case is illustrated by the color of quarks and by all properties of objects that are causally isolated from all observers in space-time. Kosso concludes that this kind of unobservability is still theory dependent. Hence unobservable in principle is not the same as absolutely unobservable. Second, objects and their properties may be unperceivable in fact. That is to say, such things can convey significant information to an apparatus but not directly to a human sense organ. This applies, for instance, to the observation of the energy of an individual photon, the form of a DNA string in a cell, and the shape and motion of tectonic plates. It is important to see that Kosso's usage of these distinctions implies that an object-property pair (for instance the shape of a DNA string) can be observable even if it is unperceivable in fact. Finally, there are the perceivable things, which can directly interact in an informative way with a human being. An example from this category is the observation of a heat flow between an object and the human body or the observation of photographs of bubble chamber tracks.

Kosso's conclusion from his case studies is that the issues of observability and observation in science are complex and diverse. To account for this complexity and diversity he introduces four different dimensions of observability. A first dimension is the degree of immediacy of scientific observability. It pertains to the three possibilities in the interaction between object, apparatus, and observer. Hence, the degree of immediacy may vary from perceivable, through unperceivable in fact, to unobservable in principle. Thus a naked eye observation is relatively immediate, while an observation that requires the use of extensive apparatuses is strongly mediated. Next, there is the directness of an observation. Along this dimension we measure the causal distance, that is, the length and the complexity of the causal chain from the object to the observing apparatus or observer. Thus observing the heat flow from an object x to an observer is quite direct, since obtaining the information requires only a single interaction between x and the body of the observer. In contrast, the observation of a photon by means of a photomultiplier is based on a long chain of different causal processes and hence is rather indirect.

A further dimension is the amount of interpretation necessary for inferring the information about the object from the perception of the end state of the apparatus. This interpretation is provided by the theoretical account of the observational process. The values along this third dimension of observability may be said to measure the epistemic distance between the states of the apparatus and the states of the observed object. The amount of interpretation may vary considerably across different observations. For instance, observing the shape or motion of a tectonic plate requires an interpretation in terms of a larger number of distinct laws than does observing a photon. An important qualification with respect to the dimension of amount of interpretation is that the relevant inference is not necessarily performed in an explicit manner by each individual observer. According to Kosso, "the inference we speak of here is that justification which is available to the epistemic community should an explicit account of the informational content be called for" (Kosso 1989, 141).

The fourth dimension is called the independence of interpretation. It measures the extent to which the theories used to account for the conveyance of information overlap with, or depend on, the theories of the things to be observed. Again, the cases show a large variety along this dimension. Thus the observation of the form of a DNA string by means of an electron microscope is much more independent than is observing an individual atom by means of the same apparatus. In the latter case, the theory of the atom to be observed is essentially involved in the theoretical account of the working of the electron microscope.

Finally, Kosso discusses the question of the epistemic significance of these four dimensions of observability. That is to say, what relevance do the various dimensions have with respect to the reliability of the information that may be acquired by means of a particular observation? Kosso (1989, 138–48) argues that immediacy, directness, and amount of interpretation do not contribute much to the epistemic reliability of our belief in the informational content of an observation. An immediate and direct observation that does not require much interpretation is not necessarily highly reliable, while a more mediate and indirect one based on substantial interpretation is not for that reason unreliable. What counts according to the interaction-information account is not causal or epistemic proximity but the quality of the inference to the source of the information. In Kosso's view, it is the independence of interpretation that provides the central epistemic norm for measuring this quality. "Since the information must be unpacked, the reliability of the unpacking must be accountable, and that accountability comes as the independence between the causal laws used in analyzing the information and the theory of the object itself. The epistemic reliability can come only with disinterest such that the theory describing observability has little or no important stake in the outcome" (Kosso 1989, 147).[1]

For example, in the case of the ethers from eighteenth- and nineteenth-century physics, ether theory and the theories that accounted for the conveyance of the information about the ethers coincided to a large extent. It is this mutual dependence that, according to Kosso, is the main reason for the implausibility of the belief in the existence of these ethers.

Problems of the Interaction-Information Account

Kosso offers a number of detailed and illuminating theoretical analyses of observational processes in terms of the interactions between objects and their properties, observing apparatuses, and human observers. His case studies convincingly demonstrate the complexity and diversity of the notions of observability and observation in scientific practice. Furthermore, the various dimensions of observability introduced and discussed by him enable a better grasp of these complicated notions.

A striking feature of Kosso's view is that he does not distinguish between observation and experiment. In fact, the majority of his cases constitute what most people would call experiments. In my own terminology, the interaction-information account of observation focuses on the theoretical description or interpretation of experimental systems. As such, it provides an illuminating account of several important aspects of this theoretical interpretation. There is a further aspect of experimentation and observation, however, that is completely absent from Kosso's account. This is the material realization of experiments and observations, their actual performance in concrete laboratory or field settings (see Radder 1988, chap. 3; 1996, chap. 2; chap. 7, below).

The notion of material realization accounts for the evident fact that observation involves more than mere theoretical interpretation. In addition, observational processes are, or have to be, brought about in the material world. Kosso's analyses, however, are restricted to theoretical representations of observational processes. Notwithstanding his subject matter, his approach clearly exemplifies a theory-dominant philosophy of science. No doubt this bias derives from the fact that, ultimately, Kosso shares the traditional view that the critical philosophical issue is the significance of observability for the epistemic status of theories. In this view, the material realization of concrete experiments and observations is simply taken for granted.

Thus, in the interaction-information account of observation, the role of human action is conspicuously absent. In this respect it does not differ from the views of Hanson, discussed in the previous chapter, and from those of Paul Churchland, which I examine in the next chapter. Typically enough, one of the very few times human action is mentioned by Kosso (in the form of the mobility of eyes and head) it comes up as a problem, and not as a resource, for making observations (in this case, of the acceleration of an object; see Kosso 1989, 116).

Several claims made by Kosso are questionable because of his neglect of the processes of materially realizing observations. Thus he agrees with Bas van Fraassen that the question of whether things are (un)observable in principle or (un)perceivable by human beings "can be handled entirely by the physical theories of the situation, the physics, biology and other sciences of the source or media" (Kosso 1989, 33). This claim, however, is hardly compatible with his empirical approach and his reliance on cases of concrete observability in science. Consider, for instance, the case of the (un)perceivability of objects by human beings. In this case, in scientific practice it often happens that some people succeed in perceiving certain objects and their properties, while others fail. That is to say, in real science the question, perceivable by whom? plays a significant role. Moreover, contrary to Kosso's claim, in most instances such variations in perceivability cannot be explained by explicit (physical or biological) theories and laws. Instead, they are usually accounted for by reference to variations in skill and training (see, for instance, Hacking 1983; Collins 1985; Gooding 1990).

A related problem bears on the issue of the noticeability of the relevant features of an observational process. Kosso claims that "the ease with which a feature is noticed, either by the trained or untrained observer, is too dramatically a product of the packaging of the instrumentation. . . . Processing the information into a noticeable form will not add more information of the object. For this reason, noticeability, while a convenient feature, is not epistemically significant" (Kosso 1989, 143).

However, if it is the case that the question, perceivable by whom? is an important issue in scientific practice, and if there are no reasons to assume that this will change within the foreseeable future, then noticeability is surely epistemically relevant. The reason is that reproducibility of observations is generally taken to be, at least, a necessary condition for the reliability of observationally acquired information. If a particular object and its properties can only be observed by a single scientist, however competent he or she is considered to be, and if other scientists consistently fail to reproduce the observation, the claimed information will be seen as epistemically dubious. Hence an important aspect of observational practices is to try to standardize observational processes in such a way that the results become more easily noticeable for a larger group of scientists (see, for example, Rouse 1987, chap. 4; Radder 1996, chap. 2).

Next, despite the important role that the interaction-information account of observability and observation attaches to theory, the philosophical consequences of this role have not been adequately dealt with. Kosso seems to assume that the main philosophical problems arising from the theory dependence of observation have been solved by his discussion of the notion of independence of interpretation. He concludes that good observations (should) have a high degree of independence, and hence he claims that independence is the most important measure of the epistemic reliability of the information acquired through observations.

Kosso's notion of independence cannot bear this epistemic burden, however, since it has some serious shortcomings. These can be demonstrated through a closer look at the way this notion has been defined. Kosso (1989, 43–49) first introduces the following notation for the theories and subtheories involved:

(i) T_x is the theory of the observable object x.

(ii) T_x1, a subtheory of T_x, is the collection of propositions for which the fact that "x is P" could be used as confirming evidence.

(iii) $\{T_i\}$ is the set of theories that is employed to account for the claim that "x is P" is being observed through the observational process in question.

(iv) T_x2 is that subtheory of T_x which is part of, or dependent on, the theories $\{T_i\}$.

With the help of these definitions, Kosso proposes a criterion for the "independence of interpretation." He states, "The measure of the independence of account will be an evaluation of both the relation between T_x1 and T_x2, *and* the relation between T_x2 and $\{T_i\}$. A high score for independence results in the case of little or no intersection of T_x1 and T_x2, and, in the same case, T_x2 playing only a minor role in the account $\{T_i\}$" (Kosso 1989, 46).

Thus it may be the case that one part of the theory-of-x (to wit, T_x2) is used to account for the observation that a certain x is P. This does not imply, though, that the crucial part of the theory—the part T_x1, for which the outcome of this observation may provide confirming evidence—is similarly presupposed in interpreting the observational process.

This criterion of independence, and Kosso's explanation of it, pose two important problems, however. The first bears on what he calls the depth of involvement of T_x2 in $\{T_i\}$. The idea is that the larger the involvement of T_x2 in $\{T_i\}$, the smaller the degree of independence. Now, suppose that we add some further links to the chain of interaction between object and observer, and suppose that these links are accounted for by theories that are independent of T_x and different from the theories T_i used so far. In this case, the addition implies an expansion of the set $\{T_i\}$ without changing $T_x 2$. For instance, instead of directly reading the temperature of a thermometer, we may make a photograph of its final state, then print the corresponding number by means of some recording device, and finally take a look at this printed number. In this way, the relative role of $T_x 2$ within the set $\{T_i\}$ will decrease and, according to the above criterion, the independence of interpretation will increase.

The point of this argument is that this addition of links to the causal chain, and of new theories to account for them, also entails a decrease of directness and an increase of amount of interpretation. Thus the latter dimensions prove to be directly related to the independence of interpretation. Hence these three dimensions of observability are not independent or orthogonal, contrary to Kosso's (1989, 143–45) claim. Consequently, not only independence but also directness and amount of interpretation should be epistemically significant.

A second problem of the criterion of independence pertains to the relationship between $T_x 1$ and $T_x 2$, as discussed by Kosso. According to him, observations for which $T_x 2$ is empty or for which $T_x 1$ and $T_x 2$ are disjoint entail the largest degree of epistemic significance. However, it is difficult to see how such cases might occur. First, on the interaction-information account, any observation will include an interaction between x and a further link in the causal chain of interactions. The account of this first interaction will be a part of $T_x 2$, and thus $T_x 2$ can never be empty. Nor can it be the case that $T_x 1$ and $T_x 2$ are disjoint. After all, they share at least one significant proposition, namely, the claim that "there is at least one x." These arguments show that the most independent relationship that may be realized between $T_x 1$ and $T_x 2$ is the case in which $T_x 1$ and $T_x 2$ display at least some overlap. Hence, according to Kosso's own classification (1989, 46–48), the optimal epistemic situation is always a situation of "theoretical nepotism"!

My conclusion is that the technical explanation of the notion of independence exhibits some important flaws. Remarkably and fortunately enough, the discussion of the various cases of scientific observability and observation (in the third chapter of Kosso's book) hardly uses the details of the systematic analysis of the notion of independence of interpretation developed in its second chapter. In promoting the notion of independence of interpretation, Kosso intends to eliminate a direct circularity between what we claim to observe and what we (epistemically) presuppose in interpreting observational processes. My criticisms of this notion imply, first, that independence alone cannot bear the entire epistemic burden and second, that full independence is impossible and hence not all circularity can be avoided.

A related problem arises when we take into account another feature of Kosso's approach. Having almost arrived at the end of his book, he apparently realized that the epistemic reliability of the information acquired through a particular observation depends not only on the independence of interpretation but also on the reliability of the theories $\{T_i\}$ that account for the observational process (Kosso 1989, 151–53). Thus a further interdependence between theory and observation is involved here, in the sense that reliable observational information depends on reliable theories of the observational process, while the reliability of these theories depends again on reliable observational information, and so on ad infinitum. Kosso briefly acknowledges the point but states that it is too large to be dealt with in the context of his discussions of observability and observation. The result is, however, that his account of the relationship between theory and observation is not only flawed but also incomplete.[2]

Finally, the existence of these direct and indirect interdependences between theory and observation casts doubt on another basic claim of the interaction-information account. Apparently, Kosso assumes that ready-made and unambiguous information somehow inheres in objects and their properties and then, given suitable interactions, flows in a unidirectional way from the objects to apparatuses and observers. "Information is transferred between states through interaction. The object in state S which has informational content (x is P) interacts with something else, the observing apparatus or some intermediate informational medium, with the result that this latter object is left in a state A which has the information (x is P) whereas it did not have that information before the interaction" (Kosso 1989, 37).

As we have seen, the content of observational information depends crucially on the (reliability of the) theories $\{T_i\}$ of the observational process.
Unfortunately, this fact is noticed by Kosso more or less as an afterthought.
However, the existence of a systematic impact of theories on the content of
observational information seems to be at odds with the objectivist account
of information Kosso advocates. According to Patrick Heelan, this ambiguity of the notion of information can be found in many information-theoretic analyses of perception. The problem is that all too often no distinction
is made between two senses of information: information as a structured
stimulus field and information as a communicated content about the world
(see Heelan 1983, 136–38).

Consider, for example, Kosso's claim (1989, 148–51) that independence
of interpretation warrants an inference to the objective existence of the
source of the information. In view of my criticisms of the interaction-information theory of observability and observation, this claim is highly questionable. Since $T_x 1$ and $T_x 2$, at best, overlap, and since they both assume
that there is at least one x, the critical issue is not their independence but
the plausibility of $T_x 2$ and, more generally, of $\{T_i\}$. The problem increases
when we take into account that, in real science, the theories of the observational process $\{T_i\}$ are liable to controversy and change. By sidestepping this
issue and by focusing instead on a questionable notion of independence of
interpretation, the full problem of the theory dependence of observation
has not been treated adequately by Kosso.

5

CONNECTIONIST ACCOUNTS OF OBSERVATION

Connectionism is an interesting, recent approach that is quite prominent in the fields of computational neuroscience, artificial intelligence, and cognitive psychology. It claims to provide an adequate account of (naturalistically conceived) observational processes. Moreover, it explicitly endorses the theory ladenness of observation. Thus, given the discussion in the preceding chapters, connectionism might be seen as a promising candidate for a plausible theory of observation. In this chapter, I examine and test this conjecture.[1]

At its most ambitious, connectionism assumes that most, or even all, cognitive achievements by humans may be successfully modeled by means of connectionist networks (also called neural networks or parallel processing networks). These achievements include sense perception, memory retrieval, concept formation and application, theoretical explanation, and logical reasoning. Weaker and stronger interpretations of what is modeled by connectionist networks can be found. Some interpreters see networks primarily as models of cognitive behavior. Others, moreover, claim that networks adequately describe the basic features of the working of the brain, and hence they speak of neural networks and a neurocomputational approach.

The significance of connectionism, both scientific and philosophical, is also assessed differently by different authors. Thus Paul Churchland (1992b) announces—with the same aplomb as the prophecies of the symbolic artificial intelligence revolution were heralded in the 1950s and 1960s—the death of the old ways of thinking and living and the victory of the new neurocomputational doctrine. In contrast, William Bechtel and Adele Abrahamsen (1991) offer a more cautious interpretation by adding appropriate caveats and showing a sense of perspective at several points in their discussion. They advocate a more pluralist approach, in which both connectionist and symbol manipulation models may play a legitimate role.[2] As in the case of any science, connectionist cognitive science does not force a unique and unambiguous philosophical interpretation on us. For this reason, my critical assessment of connectionism applies primarily to a specific (but influential) interpretation, which is called nonsentential computationalism by Terrence Horgan (1997) and which is advocated by Churchland, among others.

Before turning to philosophical issues, however, we must first examine how a connectionist network is able to perceive or observe something. Answering this question requires some explanation of the operation of connectionist networks. In general, a network consists of several layers of units. These units will be activated—that is to say, they acquire particular activation values—in the course of an observational process. A first layer contains several input units that encode the sensory input; next, one or more layers of hidden units serve to process the input information; and finally, a layer of output units contains the encoded result of the observational process. To enable the processing of activation through the network, each unit in a layer is connected to all other units in adjacent layers (hence the name connectionism). Processing involves not only a transfer but also a transformation of input information. For this purpose, each connection between units possesses a weighing mechanism. When a certain input is being processed through a certain connection, the activation value of the unit will increase, decrease, or remain the same, depending on the particular value of the weight of this connection. An important dynamic feature of networks is that their weights can be adapted in different runs so as to produce different outputs from a given input. In sum, what the network does in a particular run is to compute the output activation values on the basis of a given a set of weights and a given set of input activation values.

Next, most connectionist accounts assume that perception has to be learned. Hence network design involves two stages, a training stage and a test stage. In the training stage, the input units are assigned particular activation values that, taken together, represent a particular observable situation. This input activation is processed through the network and will thus lead to a particular activation of the output units. Then, the resulting output activation is compared to an antecedently specified desired output, which represents the correct result of the observation. For instance, if the network is to learn to distinguish between red and green objects, there might be two output units, with the activation levels {1,0} representing "red" and the levels {0,1} representing "green." In this case, the network will be successful if the input activation representing a red object consistently leads to (or approximates) the output activation levels {1,0}, while a green object (approximately) produces the activation levels {0,1}.

The procedure for obtaining the desired output state at the end of the training stage involves changing the weights of the connections in subsequent runs according to a so-called learning rule. This rule may take on different forms, but the basic idea is that, in the course of a number of runs, it changes the weights in such a way that the difference between the resulting outputs and the desired outputs becomes minimized. When this minimum has been reached, training has been completed.[3] Now the network has to be tested to see how the final weight distribution resulting from the learning process will respond to a test set of new cases of the observable situation. To date, quite a few connectionist networks have successfully passed such tests and some are being used in a commercial, technological context. Connectionist networks are claimed to be particularly good at recognizing perceptual patterns.

A further claim made by proponents of connectionism is that this approach has definitively confirmed the idea of the theory ladenness of observation, albeit in a somewhat revised manner. Bechtel and Abrahamsen (1991, 112–20, 159–63) provide a nice illustration: a network that simulates the so-called word superiority effect, the fact that having a prior "theory" about what word is being recognized affects the observation of its constituent letters. More generally, the argument for the theory ladenness of connectionist observation is as follows (Churchland 1992a, 354–55). A successful learning process will result in a specific configuration of the weights of the connections between the units of the network. Applied to new situations, this configuration will process the perceptual input activation in a specific way. Hence, if we interpret the weight configuration of a network as encoding or as determining a certain conceptual framework or a certain theory, we may say that all cognitively relevant observation is conceptually organized or theory laden. Accordingly, this connectionist interpretation subscribes to the anti-empiricist view that observation can never provide a neutral or indubitable foundation of other epistemic claims and decisions.

How to Distinguish a Rock from a Mine

A concrete case may make all this more tangible. Consider the task of discriminating between sonar echoes reflected from two different kinds of undersea targets, namely, submarine mines and submarine rocks. The original source of this case is R. Paul Gorman and Terrence Sejnowski (1988), but I start by reviewing the account provided by Churchland (1989, 163–71; 1992a, 343–53). He emphasizes the difficulty of the task, resulting from the fact that echoes of different kinds of object are hardly distinguishable by the human ear, while echoes of the same kind show considerable variation. He describes the procedure as follows. "We begin by recording fifty different mine echoes and fifty different rock echoes, a fair sample of each. We then digitize the power profile of each echo with a frequency analyzer, and feed the resulting vector into the bank of input units. . . . We want the output units to respond with appropriate activation levels (specifically {1,0} for a mine; {0,1} for a rock) when fed an echo of either kind" (1992a, 345–46).

One of the networks put to this task is a three-layered network, having thirteen input units, seven hidden units, and two output units (see the upper part of figure 5.1). After the learning process has been finished, the network proves to be able to identify new rock and mine echoes in a remarkably reliable way. Churchland stresses the autonomous and spontaneous working of the network. "Here we have a binary discrimination between a pair of diffuse and very hard-to-define acoustic properties. Indeed, we never did define them! It is the network that has generated an appropriate internal characterization of each type of sound, fueled only by examples" (Churchland 1992a, 346).

Moreover, the successes of connectionist networks are claimed to support a physicalist and reductionist philosophical position. The philosophically important question, to be answered in the next section, is whether this claim can be justified. For this purpose, I first examine the rock-mine example in more detail.

What needs to be done to make these rock-mine observations? Much more is required than what is taken into account by Churchland. Moreover, even Gorman and Sejnowski's analysis will be seen to be incomplete in certain critical respects. The following seven-step account of the observational process is still sketchy, but it at least lays out the requisite ingredients. It begins with the input side.

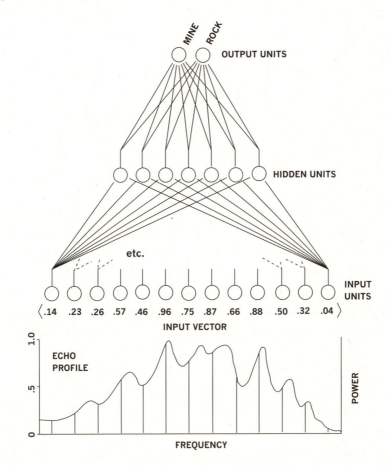

FIGURE 5.1. Input and structure of the rock-mine network. Reproduced from Churchland (1989, 165).

1. Initially, a seaworthy ship (or perhaps a submarine) including the relevant detection instruments has to be acquired, and a capable crew as well as some experienced scientists and technicians have to be recruited. Then, the ship sails to a chosen test location on the open sea.

2. Upon arrival, the observational process has to be staged. The required instruments must be set up by the scientists and technicians and be tested for normal operation. Then, the first target (a metal cylinder representing a mine) is to be positioned on the sea floor. This might be done, for instance, by some professional divers who take part in the expedition. Subsequently, a set of auditory "mine" echoes will be recorded. The echoes are taken at a variety of angles to produce a number of different recordings. Next, the divers must remove the "mine" and replace it by a cylindrically shaped "rock." Finally, an analogous set of auditory rock echoes from various angles will be recorded. From this brief sketch it will be clear that making scientific observations involves a variety of different activities, even in the case of relatively standardized observations such as the recording of sonar echoes.[4]

3. The next step is to further process the recorded sound profiles. First, the audible echoes must be transformed by a frequency analyzer into a frequency-power diagram (see the lower part of figure 5.1, and Gorman and Sejnowski 1988, 1136–37). This diagram shows, for a particular echo, the power of the sound waves for every frequency that is present in the spectrum of the waves. Thus what happens in this step is the quantification of the qualitative auditory observation. Furthermore, a particular selection process takes place. Not every measurement recording is appropriate. A set of "good" data must be selected on the basis of, among other things, the strength of the reflected sound waves. Returns that are too weak, or returns that are seen as weird in some other respects, are eliminated as being noise.

A further step involves the discretization of the frequencies. Because the network has been designed with a limited number of input units, the continuous power profiles are statistically averaged in a certain way to obtain a finite number of power values—namely, thirteen—for each particular sonar echo. The subsequent step consists of the normalization of the power values. Because the network operates with activation values lying between 0 and 1, the values are rescaled to the interval [0,1], with 0 denoting zero power and 1 denoting maximum power. Finally, these normalized power values are transformed into dimensionless numbers. This transformation may be called the deconceptualization step. For instance, a normalized power value of 0.73 watt now simply becomes the number 0.73. It is the latter set of numbers that is fed into the network as the input vector.

So much for the input side; next is the output side and the work that has to be done there.

4. The first thing to note is that the number of output units of the network has been fixed in advance by its design. In the rock-mine example we have two output units, which means that the human designers have given the "pupil" a hint: there are two types of pattern to be distinguished (and not, for instance, five). Thus the designers have fixed the dimension of what, in network design, is called the solution space. In doing so, they have in fact predefined a crucial feature of the type of solution that is being sought.

5. Furthermore, the network itself does not know the source of its input (rock or mine). Hence evaluating whether or not a particular output is correct, or improving, requires an externally imposed norm. This normative intervention has been realized through a built-in "teacher" that assigns a desired output to each particular input. For instance, when a mine pattern has been fed in and the output vector increases in two subsequent runs from {0.73, 0.12} to {0.81, 0.09}, this teacher gives another hint by saying, "Go on, you are moving in the right direction." In this way, the learning process is supervised by the external norm of what the outcome of the network should be. The same conclusion applies to the testing process. In this way, the desired outputs entail a predefined direction of the learning and testing process.

6. Connectionist networks share a notable feature with human observers. Just like human observers, networks may recognize a pattern in a small, an average, or a large number of cases, but usually they will not be successful in all of the cases. A minimum requirement is that they should do better than chance. But how much better? To answer this question, we need an external reference point that functions as a criterion of degree of success. Churchland claims that network performance in the rock-mine case is much better than even skilled human observation. Thus he asserts that "the discrimination of such echoes poses a serious problem because they are effectively indistinguishable by the human ear" (Churchland 1992a, 345).

On this issue there is, however, a remarkable contrast between Gorman and Sejnowski's claims and Churchland's rendering of these claims. Indeed, Gorman and Sejnowski (1988, 1139–40) write, "Three human subjects were trained to classify the same two targets. . . . The average performance of the three trained human listeners was 91 percent. The performance of the networks, trained on preprocessed versions of the signals, was close to 100 percent." They note the incomplete character of the comparison between human and network performance, but their provisional conclusion is that the improvement through networks is primarily an improvement over alternative automated classifiers. Be that as it may, the point is that without an external reference, the question, how good is good enough? remains unanswerable. Put in more technical terms, such an external criterion allows us to finish the training stage at a definite point, even if we do not know whether the network has reached an optimal error minimum or whether it has settled into a merely local error minimum that might be decreased by increasing the size of the training set.

7. Like the input activation values, the output activation values are mere numbers. To know what has been observed, these numbers have to be semantically interpreted. Because of the deconceptualization during the input stage, a corresponding conceptualization during the output stage is required (compare with Meijsing 1993, 60–65). Thus the output pattern {1,0} must be interpreted as "mine" or "a mine is observed." Obviously, this

conceptual quality has not been perceived by the network itself, but has been assigned to a particular set of output vectors by its designers or users.

What Networks Cannot Do, and What They Can

According to many connectionists, networks can learn to discriminate between complex perceptual features, and thus they are said to be able to acquire real perceptual knowledge. Churchland, moreover, uses the successes of connectionist networks to support his physicalist and reductionist philosophical position. As to physicalism, he claims, "And yet it is a purely physical system that recognizes such intricacies. Short of appealing to magic, or of simply refusing to confront the problem at all, we must assume that some configuration of purely physical elements is capable of grasping and manipulating these features, and by means of purely physical principles" (1989, 164). And about reductionism he states, "What the reductionist must do is explain how a physical system can come to address and manipulate such subtle and culturally configured features. While this is certainly a challenge, it no longer appears to be a problem in principle, for we have already seen how suitably trained networks can come to represent and discriminate features of great subtlety and abstraction" (132–33).

Several rather strong claims are made here about the perceptual accomplishments of physical, connectionist networks. The main objective of the final section of this chapter is to evaluate these and related claims. Hence the focus is on Churchland's views. For the purpose of this evaluation, I use both the more general conclusions obtained in the discussion of Hanson's account of observation (summarized at the end of chapter 3) and the more specific results of the analysis of the rock-mine observational process in the previous section.

The first conclusion drawn from the discussion in chapter 3 is that unmediated observation, which might provide an exclusive foundation of knowledge, does not exist. Churchland explicitly subscribes to this conclusion. He states, for example, that "there can be no question of grounding all epistemic decisions in some neutral observation framework" (Churchland 1992a, 355). More specifically, all observation is conceptually interpreted.

On this issue, proponents of connectionism appear to agree. For instance, Churchland (354–55) claims that Paul Feyerabend's views on theory ladenness have been vindicated within a neurocomputational perspective when we identify the theory that structures a particular observation with a specific set of partitions on the activation space of a particular neural network.

Yet Churchland's account of theory ladenness cannot be accepted as it stands, since it includes some additional but questionable claims. First, as we have seen in chapter 3, it is preferable to speak consistently of conceptual interpretation instead of theory ladenness, because not all concepts that structure our observations can be naturally identified as (scientific) theories. Next, Churchland's identification of concepts with specific, physical systems has been criticized by various authors (Glymour 1992; Fodor and Lepore 1996, 159–62; Kirschenmann 1996). In part 2 of this book, I return to this issue and argue that a concept possesses an abstract meaning, and hence it cannot be reduced to a purely physical object. A final problem derives from Churchland's more general views on theory ladenness. He claims that the theory ladenness of observation has three important implications. "We must direct our attention away from foundational epistemologies. . . . Our current observational ontology is just one such ontology out of an indefinitely large number of alternative observational ontologies. . . . Since some theoretical frameworks are markedly superior to others, the quality of our observational knowledge is in principle improvable" (Churchland 1989, 255).

However, although the first claim is correct, the other two are questionable. The second claim—which suggests that real people are indefinitely plastic—has been rightly criticized by Jerry Fodor (1984), while the last one assumes a controversial notion of theoretical progress (for some criticisms, see Radder 1996, chap. 3). Furthermore, in contrast to what Churchland suggests, the latter two claims are by no means "direct consequences" of theory ladenness, since they require substantive additional premises. Proponents of the view that observation is theory laden (or better, conceptually interpreted) need not be committed to these additional premises.

What then are the implications of my account of the rock-mine network?

This rock-mine example plays a substantial role in Churchland's argumentation, and it is fairly representative as a connectionist model of human observation. My critical evaluation employs the method of systematically uncovering the human contributions to the cognitive tasks in question.[5]

First we have seen that, in Hanson's terminology, all observation involves seeing-as and often also seeing-that. From this it follows that a network on its own cannot be said to see or observe anything. Consider the successive steps in the analysis of the observational process of distinguishing between mines and rocks. Seeing that a pattern is a mine or seeing a certain pattern as distinctively rocklike depends essentially on additional achievements (particularly, on steps 3 and 7), which are not the result of the operation of the network.

More specifically, the analysis demonstrates that more knowledge is involved in making these rock-mine observations than that which is encoded in the set of connection weights of the network. After all, correctly seeing a certain output pattern as either a rock or a mine requires at least a knowledge of the fact that the relevant pattern is the causal effect of something like the observational process sketched in step 2. Again, this kind of knowledge has not resulted from the operation of the network itself. Remarkably enough, even the original paper by Gorman and Sejnowski tells us nothing about the realization of the processes from which the sonar echo data result, and it does not contain a single reference to relevant publications on these observational processes. Apparently, the data are treated as being, literally, "given." However, how can the network be said to have observed patterns of mines or rocks, if it is unknown by whom or by what the data have been given?

At issue here is an important aspect of present-day scientific practice, to wit the ubiquity of processes of division of labor in the production of scientific knowledge. This division of scientific labor requires a reliable coordination of the various steps of the observational process. The usual solution to this coordination problem relies on professional or moral codes and institutional arrangements. The function of these codes and arrangements is to warrant the competence and credibility of scientists. Hence, generally speaking, individual scientists may be assured that the "given" data really originate from competently performed experiments and that the results have been reported in a reliable way. Such coordinating mechanisms do not exist in the case of networks. Moreover, sidestepping the problem by simply postulating the abstract possibility of functionally equivalent procedures, which could be carried out by future networks, will not do for the naturalistic philosopher. Although such a move is not unusual, it is more suitable for speculative science fiction than for a scientifically conceived philosophy.

This discussion also bears on the further claim that connectionism may be the clue to the solution of the problem of the intentionality of mental states. "The connectionist approach to modeling cognition thus offers promise in explaining the *aboutness* or *intentionality* of mental states. Representational states, especially those of hidden units, constitute the system's own learned response to inputs. Since they constitute the system's adaptation to the input, there is a clear respect in which they would be *about* objects or events in the environment if the system were connected, via sensory-motor organs, to such an environment" (Bechtel and Abrahamsen 1991, 129).

In fact the reverse conclusion appears to be more plausible. A network itself encodes only a tiny fraction of the particular observational process, and it is only marginally involved in the interaction with a particular environment. Therefore, any explanation of intentionality should be expected to go far beyond the operation of networks by taking account of the additional human contributions that are necessary to realize the relevant observational processes.[6]

A further major conclusion from the previous chapters emphasizes the indispensability of human action, in the form of movements of body parts, locomotion, or intervention. Steps 1 and 2, in particular, testify to the significance of these nonlinguistic factors for the rock-mine observational process. Since establishing the desired output means being able to know in advance which input patterns originate from rocks and which from mines, the locomotion of the divers as well as their actions in adequately positioning the mines and the rocks constitutes a critical aspect of the observational process. Also, taking measurements from different angles may well require skillful experimental action, especially when the undersea targets are located at great depth. The indispensability of action provides a further reason why networks cannot be said to possess autonomous observational capabilities.

Related to this is another issue. At some points, Churchland underlines the pragmatic virtues of successfully operating networks (1989, 221; 1992b, 478). Thus he claims that appropriately working networks will have greater "survival value" and will lead to more "rewards" and fewer "disappointments," as compared to less successful neural nets. By my analysis of connectionist observations, however, appealing to such evolutionary and behavioral mechanisms proves to be inappropriate. Consider, for instance, the procedures of normalization and deconceptualization as performed in step 3 of the rock-mine observational process. Normalized values tell us nothing about the total amount of the power of the reflected sound waves. In particular, we do not know whether the waves are high powered—and hence possibly damaging to the observing network—or whether we are dealing with harmless, low-power waves. Furthermore, deconceptualization entails the loss of all information on the nature of the phenomena we are observing. For instance, on the basis of a dimensionless input vector, we cannot know whether the input signal consists of dangerous radioactive radiation or of innocuous sound waves. This clearly shows the practical significance of the conceptualization step.[7] Consequently, important aspects of the survival value of successful observations cannot be attributed to the working of the networks themselves, even if their functioning is entirely satisfactory otherwise.

Lastly, consider the following general response to the arguments that successful operation of the networks is essentially dependent on a variety of human contributions. Of course, the connectionist might reply, it is the case that, in its learning stage, a network depends on the guidance of some outside teacher. In this respect, however, a network does not differ from a human pupil. The point is that, once the external teaching has been completed and successfully internalized, all subsequent observations can be justly attributed to the trainees themselves, whether they are human beings or connectionist networks (see also Haugeland 1987, 10–12).

Unfortunately, this argument does not hold for the case under discussion. The problem is that several of the human contributions outlined above—in particular, steps 1, 2, and 3—are not learned and internalized at all by the networks. That is to say, these steps play a role beyond the training and testing stage; they must be repeated in every new rock-mine observation process.

In sum, these arguments show that, by themselves, connectionist networks do not possess genuine observational capabilities. They are able to make successful observations because they are embedded in human material and social practices. Remarkably enough, in his reply to Fodor, Churchland himself stresses the significance of motor behavior (1989, 262–63) and of practice and socialization (264). I fail to see how this can be consistent with a neurophysiological reductionism, which is his bottom-line position.[8] I conclude, elaborating on Norwood Hanson's statement, that not only eyeballs, but also brains and brainlike networks, are blind: it is only people who are able to see (given certain material and social practices).

Finally, my critical analyses should not be taken to imply that nothing may be gained from including connectionist networks within human observational practices. For example, routine inclusion of the rock-mine network in the practice of assessing sonar echoes may well lead to definite improvements. Actually, what this network offers is a sophisticated, generalizable fitting procedure. In an iterative process, it establishes a generalizable fit between certain meaningless input and output codes. In the rock-mine case, routine inclusion of the network will entail the standardization of a (small) part of the observational process. As a consequence, this process may become less sensitive to specific human skills and more reliable in terms of stable outcomes.

A HERMENEUTICAL APPROACH TO PERCEPTION

Among my arguments against reductionist interpretations of connectionist networks are the role of division of labor in making scientific observations and the significance of professional or moral codes and institutional arrangements for reliably realizing observational processes. In more general terms, conceptions of observation exclusively in terms of the activities of isolated individuals are, at best, incomplete. By assuming that observation is always rooted in a common life world, hermeneutical approaches take a similar position.

Patrick Heelan (1983, 1989) has developed a comprehensive, hermeneutical theory of perception, which is interesting in its own right and illustrates the significance of the social dimension of perception. Heelan employs insights gained in the phenomenological and hermeneutical tradition of Edmund Husserl, Maurice Merleau-Ponty, and Martin Heidegger for the purpose of developing a detailed philosophical interpretation of the nature, the role, and the results of our acts of perception. In this way, he intends to integrate their natural and human dimensions. Although he makes certain differentiations between perception in everyday life and scientific observation, he does not oppose them as essentially different in a philosophical sense. For this reason, he clearly goes beyond earlier phenomenological and hermeneutical authors, such as Husserl, Merleau-Ponty, and Heidegger, who intended to make an explicit and value-laden philosophical contrast between "abstract" science and our "concrete" life world.

Heelan makes two intriguing general claims. First, he advocates the primacy of perception in science: the aim of science is to acquire perceptual knowledge of phenomena rather than theoretical knowledge of underlying mechanisms. Second, he argues that ordinary space perception is not necessarily and not always Euclidean. A major aim of his hermeneutical analysis is to show the significance and legitimacy of hyperbolic space perception in everyday life.

Heelan's interpretation includes an account of (what I call) the observational process. He emphasizes the necessity of "preparation": any individual act of perception requires a skillful subject, a specifically structured setting, and an appropriate cultural context. In general terms, he describes this complex observational process as follows. "In any model of perception, the sensory system (comprising the psychological and somatic processes of perception) is prepared in some way to 'resonate' in response to an appropriate light structure specific to a physical object in its background in the World: the 'tuning' of a 'resonance' to a specific stimulus is the product of learning based on the abilities of the subject, the structures of the environment, and the cultural milieu within which perception is learned" (1983, 147).

The act of perception can be logically decomposed into a physical and a cognitive moment. The two moments, however, do not refer to distinct stages or components in the real world, since they are inseparable dimensions of one and the same process. The physical moment accounts for the physical object and the somatic information processes, that is, the causal processes (physical and neurophysiological) that are going on during the perceptual act. The cognitive moment accounts for the content of the perceptual act. According to Heelan (1983, 132–34) this content is not to be found in certain intermediate entities, such as "sense data" or "ideas," out of which objects would then be constructed. Instead, he insists on the irreducibility of intentionality: the content of a perception coincides with the perceptual object. What we perceive is a state of the World and not just a representation of such a state. In line with the phenomenological and hermeneutical tradition, the gap between subject and object is being bridged by identifying the intended and the perceptual object. Furthermore, Heelan's account accords with Norwood Hanson's view of seeing-as and seeing-that, as essentially involving linguistically expressible belief, judgment, and knowledge. "I take *perception* to be a completed act of knowing, and so to be a perceptual recognition, judgment, or belief capable of being expressed in a descriptive statement about a state of the World, usually by the perceiver himself/herself" (Heelan 1983, 131).

Next, Heelan explains the cognitive moment of the act of perception in more detail. Following Husserl, he distinguishes between the outer and the inner horizon of a perception. First, any act of perception requires a distinction between a foregrounded object and a background against which the object appears. The object has to appear within an "outer horizon." After all, an object that has exactly the same color as its background and does not cast any shadow (such as the well-known white mouse in the snow) will not be perceivable. Second, at any moment an individual perceiver is always and necessarily situated at a particular location. Hence in any particular instance the object manifests itself in a specific "profile." Yet a specific profile is meaningful only in so far as, and because, it is systematically related to other possible profiles of the perceptual object. "The manifold of different possible profiles is the inner horizon of an object (of *this* object or of an object of *this* kind). These profiles exhibit the various facets of the object; the essence of the object is the set of invariant structures that generate the manifolds of its profiles" (1983, 134).

The intuitive idea is that we may look at some thing from different angles and still perceive the same object. Even if our visual sensations are not the same, an identical object manifests itself through different profiles. Moreover, the supposition is that, in the case of a genuine perception, there is an invariant, organizing structure that generates the set of possible profiles. This structure, which may be discovered by critical analysis and experimentation on the possible profiles, is called the essence of the perceptual object.

With this account, Heelan (1983, 7; 1989, 297–300) follows Husserl in his attempt to geometrize perception. Husserl suggested that the set of possible profiles is constituted by a defining structure or law. The idea is taken from mathematics and mathematical physics. A simple example is a mathematical sphere that remains invariant under the transformation group of all rotations around its center. In this case, the rotation group may be said to constitute the underlying structure or law that generates the set of all possible profiles of the sphere. An interesting feature of these symmetry transformations is that they can be applied equally to the object (a rotation of the sphere itself) or to the coordinate frame from which the object is being considered (a rotation of the perceiver). Husserl called the study of such essences, based on the analogy between mathematics and perception, the method of profile variation. "In this he established the reciprocity between initiatives of the perceiver to explore new profiles of the object (this is a dynamic subjective structure which he called 'noesis'), and the organization of changes in the object (this is an objective time ordered structure which he called 'noema')" (Heelan 1989, 299).

Clearly, profile variation "on the initiative of the perceiver" requires spatiotemporal motion. Hence a central element of the "dynamic subjective structure" is the possibility of locomotion and, more generally, human action, that is to say, the possibility of interacting with and intervening in the world. Thus we reach the same conclusion as is drawn in the previous chapters: taking account of human action is essential to understanding the process and results of human perception.

Furthermore, perceptual acts can be meaningful and successful only if they are situated in a particular context, called a World, which provides the required preunderstanding for correctly performing the perceptual act. Different sociocultural environments (may) constitute different Worlds. Hence the essence of an object is not an abstract form or an ahistorical substance, since it exists only as the organizing principle of a manifold of profiles that manifest themselves within the context of a particular, historical World. Finally, in line with the views of Merleau-Ponty and Heidegger, Heelan emphasizes the embodiment of the perceiving subject. The human subject as a perceiver is an experienced "Body," a being-in-the-World, who is both physically and intentionally engaged in this World.

The latter point is exploited by Heelan in his account of scientific observation (1983, chap. 11). Here the focus is on instrumentally mediated measurements of scientific entities and their properties. The claim is that such measurement observations—for instance, an observation of the thermodynamic temperature of an object by means of a thermometer—are not essentially different from ordinary perceptions. In both cases a Body is involved, the only difference being that in the former case the embodied perception makes use of an instrument that functions as an extension of the human sensory system, as a part of the subject's Body. Measuring instruments merely constitute a new embodiment for the scientific observer. As such, they function as a window that enables a direct perception of objects in a World. "The presence or absence of a technological element . . . does not change the essential structure of the perceptual act, neither with respect to its phenomenological characteristics, for example, of directness, nor with respect to the physical and causal relationships between the embodied perceiver and the object of the perceptual horizon" (210–11).

In this view, the entities and properties of theoretical science, which are usually said to be unobservable and merely indirectly detectable through instruments, are claimed to be directly perceivable for an embodied observer living in a relevant, technologically extended World.[1]

Moreover, the thesis of the primacy of perception implies that perceptual knowledge is the only form of really valid knowledge. Entities and properties that are in principle unperceivable, in the sense explained above, are also in principle unknowable. In some formulations, Heelan's claims even imply that "unperceivable" entails "unreal." He writes, for instance, that reality "is exactly what Worlds make manifest (or purport to make manifest) to human perceivers" (1983, 174). Elsewhere, however, he assigns a role to things-in-themselves, as "the necessary preconditions of all Worlds, of all cultures, and consequently, of human embodied subjectivity itself" (213).

At the level of philosophical principles, Heelan strongly emphasizes the hermeneutical character of his position (1983, 194–97). Traditionally, the aim of hermeneutics has been to develop interpretations of human achievements, not only of written texts but also of other symbolic expressions, such as works of art or ritual practices. The process of interpreting— or understanding, reading, making sense—presupposes a so-called fore-structure. The fore-structure enables a first reading of the text, but it is also being transformed in the process as a result of a better understanding of what the text says. This interpretative back and forth movement between fore-structure and text is called the hermeneutical circle.

Following a Heideggerian account of the hermeneutical circle, Heelan specifies three different parts of the fore-structure of understanding.[2] First, a framework of linguistic categories is needed, in which the meaning of the text can be described. Next, a set of practices and skills is required, which derive from the embodiment of the interpreter and which enable an understanding of the relationship between the text and what it refers to. A final prerequisite is a particular hypothesis that can be provisionally applied to the text to initiate the hermeneutical process.

Next, Heelan proposes to apply hermeneutics beyond its traditional domain by interpreting acts of scientific observation as "readings" of a "text" (always noted in quotation marks). Thus he takes the "reading" of the temperature from a thermometer in a literal sense. The position of the mercury column with respect to the graduated scale is the "text," which may be "read" by an observer. "The response of an instrument, which I refer to as a 'text,' shares in the information-theoretic aspect of literary texts. A 'text,' however, is 'written' by the ambient environment on a standard instrument under standard circumstances in standard signs, and is controlled by physical causality; a text is written in a standard vocabulary, syntax, and so on by a writer, and is controlled by a causality guided by the writer's intentions" (1983, 197).

In this way, the scientific instrument is interpreted as being a "readable technology."[3] Perceptual reading is a hermeneutical process that involves a fore-structure of theoretical categories, observational practices and skills, and a particular interpretation of what the "text" says. Hence the indispensability of a fore-structure entails, among other things, that all scientific observations are essentially theory laden (Heelan 1983, 202–4).

Of course, it may be difficult and take considerable time to acquire an adequate "reading" of a "text." Yet once a "text" has been familiarized, the clues of the observational process "drop out of consciousness," just as the characters and syllables do in ordinary reading. As the metaphor of instruments as windows on the world entails, a skillful perceptual "reading" results in a transparency of the content of the "text." We do not notice the window—that is, the instrument—anymore but directly see the perceptual object. However, because any perceptual reading depends on the fore-structure of a particular World and a particular Body, its outcome is never unique, absolute, or final. Through a differently situated hermeneutical process, different perceptual objects could be made manifest.

The Perception and Nature of Visual Space

The prime application and illustration of Heelan's general account of perception bears upon the perception and nature of visual space. His central claim is that, although we usually experience our environment as an (infinite) Euclidean space, we may—and occasionally we do—experience it as a finite hyperbolic space. Evidence for this claim can be found not only in the occurrence of visual illusions and in pictorial practices in the history of art, but also in the perception of everyday phenomena. For instance, an extended horizontal plane of clouds in the sky will be seen as an arched but slightly flattened surface resting on the horizon (see figure 6.1).

The crucial point is that in the case of Euclidean vision the context of both perceived object and perceiver differs from the case of hyperbolic vision.

> For a World to appear Euclidean to a visual observer, it must . . . be virtually populated with familiar (stationary) standards of length and distance, and be equipped with instantaneous means for communicating information about coincidences from all parts of space to the localized visual observer, wherever he/she happens to be.

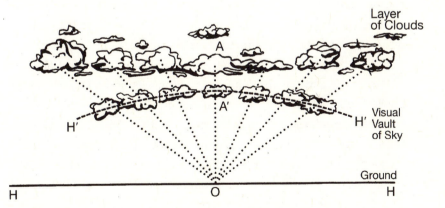

FIGURE 6.1. Visual vault of the heavens (*H'A'H'*) as it would appear if there were a horizontal layer of clouds in the sky. Reproduced from Heelan (1983, 69).

For a situation to provide a hyperbolic perceptual opportunity, the visual observer must be able to use the rule of congruence which, it is claimed, is embodied in the capacity of the unaided visual system to order the sizes, depths and distances of all objects in the unified spatial field of vision. This is done by purely visual estimation. (Heelan 1983, 51)

In contrast to Euclidean space, in hyperbolic space the perceived character of the object (particularly its shape, size, and speed) depends on, and varies with, the specific location of each individual perceiver. In the language of the phenomenological tradition, Heelan therefore speaks of a first-person account of perception. His claim is that, from both an epistemological and a cultural perspective, this kind of perception is at least as significant and legitimate as Euclidean perception. Actually, hyperbolic vision is claimed to be a more natural and more fundamental mode of experiencing a World than is Euclidean vision. According to Heelan, the latter is an artifact of our scientific culture (1983, chap. 14). While hyperbolic vision is unaided, Euclidean vision depends on the presence of fixed frames of reference and rigid rulers that are transportable through space and thus enable a universally valid, physical measurement of distance. In our scientific culture, these frames and rulers have been realized in the form of widely dispersed, engineered artifacts, such as buildings shaped as boxes, roads of constant width, cars and trains of standardized sizes, and the like. These artifacts constitute a readable technology that has become normative for the way we perceive (objects in) space. Thus our "scientifically carpentered environment" induces us to "read" the structure of visual space as being Euclidean.

From a normative point of view, Heelan advocates a (greater) plurality of Worlds. He criticizes the dominance of the scientific paradigm and the implied notion of the observer as a Cartesian, disembodied spectator, who is able to move freely within an essentially infinite, Euclidean World. Instead, he argues that this one Euclidean World should be complemented by a plurality of hyperbolic Worlds, which he characterizes as person related, locally structured, and using little standardized technology (1983, 256–62).[4] It is his basic conviction that such a synthesis of different but complementary Worlds is both possible and desirable.

Evaluating the Hermeneutics of Perception

Several elements of Heelan's account are in direct agreement with conclusions reached in the preceding chapters.[5] I have already pointed out the correspondence between Heelan's interpretation of perception as an act of knowing and the account of perception in terms of seeing-as and seeing-that. In particular, the idea of perception as concept dependent fits in well with the hermeneutical notion of a fore-structure. Furthermore, even if he does not offer a detailed account of the physical moment of the perceptual act, Heelan explicitly acknowledges its significance. Moreover, in contrast to connectionist authors, he expressly argues against the reduction of perception to a purely natural process by emphasizing the indispensability of the cognitive moment of the perceptual act.

Some of Heelan's further claims, however, are more questionable. A first issue bears upon the idea of experience as the foundation of knowledge. In many empiricist doctrines of perception, the required foundation is assumed to be ahistorical and universally valid. In this respect, my criticisms of such doctrines in the previous chapters do not apply to Heelan's account. Yet in another respect Heelan's hermeneutical interpretation may be questioned. Consider, for example, his claims on "certainty" and "apodicticity" for perceptual judgments (1983, 134–35). These claims make sense only because he conceives of perception as always embedded in an apparently given, well-developed, and seamless World. What is lacking is a satisfactory analysis of rising or changing Worlds and of controversies or clashes within and between Worlds (see also Fuller 1988, 126–27). In this sense, the Euclidean and the hyperbolic Worlds are being abstractly opposed to each other, while their historical interactions are left largely unanalyzed.

A related notion is direct perception and the idea of the essence of a perceptual object. Certainly, it is correct that perceiving an object cannot be reduced to the perception of any finite number of individual profiles of that object. In this sense, the idea of relating the object to the set of possible profiles appears to be on the right track. Heelan's specific development of this idea, however, is not fully convincing. Heelan adopts the method of profile variation that Husserl derived from mathematics and mathematical physics. A prime example is (the perception of) a mathematically ideal sphere, in which case the group of all rotations around its center generates the set of all possible profiles, and hence the structure of this group constitutes the essence of the (perceived) sphere.

Heelan's use of the analogy between mathematics and perception gives rise to certain problems, though. These problems are due to the fact that, in a number of ways, profile variation in mathematical transformations differs from profile variation in perceptual acts. First, in perceptual practice the claimed reciprocity between movements of the perceiver and changes of the object does not always obtain. As I note in the discussion of the picture of the bear climbing up the other side of a tree in chapter 3, in the case of fixed objects (such as a hill or a house), the only option is to explore new profiles on the initiative of the perceiver. Thus, while in mathematical practice there is an unrestricted freedom to vary the profiles through changes on the side of both object and subject, in perceptual practice the required freedom to realize various profiles applies primarily to the observing subject. Second, it is a characteristic of the perceived profiles of an object that they all are different, whereas all mathematical "profiles" generated by a transformation group are exactly identical.

Related to this is a third problem: in contrast to the structures or laws that underlie mathematical symmetry transformations, the existence of the essence of a perceptual object cannot be strictly proven. Instead, it appears to result from a kind of abductive inference from the set of possible profiles. Unfortunately, Heelan does not explain the nature of this inference. He asserts, for instance, that some claimed essences (e.g., of the perceptual object "phlogiston") may turn out to be pseudoessences, but he does not spell out the grounds for this assertion (1983, 135–36, 228–29).[6] These three points imply that the analogy with mathematical transformations is only partially helpful in explaining the content of perceptual acts. Some further argument is required for the claim that we directly perceive objects, and not just individual profiles, and that these perceived objects possess an essence.

I think that this further argument should take into account the conceptual interpretation of perceptual acts. Our perceiving of objects, rather than bundles of profiles, is to be explained on the basis of the intrinsic relation between the material realization and the conceptual interpretation of perceptual acts. Although Heelan explicitly acknowledges the role of interpretation in realizing perceptual acts, he does not discuss the question of precisely how those interpretations organize the actual processes of profile variation into a perceived object. Having an answer to this question, however, is crucial for understanding and assessing the phenomenological and hermeneutical thesis of the identity of intended and perceptual object. In part 2 of this book, I return to this issue of how and to what extent concepts, including the conceptual interpretations of observational processes, structure the objects of our world.

Further problems bear upon the relation between the method of profile variation and the theory of hyperbolic vision. The method of profile variation entails the importance of human action as an indispensable dimension of the perceptual act. In addition, for the case of scientific observation in a laboratory setting, Heelan points to the "preparation by a standard procedure" as an important method for making perceptual objects manifest (1989, 297). One problem is, however, that this part of Heelan's views appears to be incompatible with the interpretation of hyperbolic vision as the most natural mode of experiencing a World. Surely, in this interpretation the embodiment of the observer plays a distinctive role. Yet claiming a role for embodiment as such does not amount to a recognition of the full significance of human action. Consider the following arguments.

A general characteristic of hyperbolic space is that the shape, size, and speed of objects depends on the location of the individual perceiver. As one illustration, Heelan (1983, 114–28) discusses Vincent van Gogh's painting *Bedroom at Arles*.

Heelan claims that Van Gogh's pictorial space should be seen as a finite hyperbolic visual space, viewed from the position of the painter. From this position, the shapes and sizes of the objects in the room are distorted, as compared to the results of a Euclidean perceptual act. The corners of both the room and the bed, for instance, are not at right angles, as they are on a Euclidean view.

But is it really true that "to be at home in Euclidean horizons, is not . . . necessary for the general public" (Heelan 1983, 259)? Imagine that the

FIGURE 6.2. Vincent Van Gogh, *The Bedroom,* 1888. Available at http://www. vangoghmuseum.nl/collection/catalog (Van Gogh Museum, Amsterdam).

bedroom at Arles is your home. In a furniture shop you have bought a rectangular bed to replace the one painted by Van Gogh along the right wall of the room. Having arrived at the painter's position you put together the parts of the bed. You then take a look inside the room. At this point, you will suddenly realize that your purchase is a complete failure and that the rectangular bed does not fit at all, unless you are "at home in Euclidean horizons" and are thus familiar with the fact that, at the planned position of the bed, the shape of the room is Euclidean.

To extend the tale somewhat further, suppose that the room is being occupied by you and your partner. One day, you agree that the one of you will make a new table and the other a matching chair. Your partner and you estimate the required sizes and shapes on the basis of hyperbolic perceptions from two clearly different positions. Unfortunately, after having finished the two pieces of furniture, you discover that the resulting table and chair do not match at all. Thus, if we want to be successful in coordinating the perceptions and the instrumental actions of differently situated observers, Euclidean vision appears to be requisite.[7] What this shows is that an exclusive reliance on hyperbolic vision will hinder an adequate communication and coordination among different observers. In terms of Heelan's phenomenological terminology, the moral of my development of the *Bedroom at Arles* example is that "first-person" accounts of perception should not be limited to the singular *I* but should include the plural *we*.

Several conclusions follow from this simple example. First, the claim that Euclidean vision is no more than an artifact of our scientific culture proves to be implausible.[8] This is certainly the case for finite Euclidean space. People made successful uses of all kinds of transportable Euclidean objects long before the rise of modern science. In other words, the craftsmanship of the *homo faber* does not presuppose the (more theoretical) achievements of the (scientific) homo sapiens.

Heelan might reply that the above examples essentially presuppose a technologically carpentered environment, even if they have no necessary bearing on modern science. Thus, he writes, "In untouched Nature, among mountains and in wild places, in sea and sky, beyond the domains populated with visually accessible Euclidean standards, the geometrical structure of visual space may become indeterminate, or more likely may tend toward the hyperbolic" (1983, 252).

Yet even this claim is too strong. Consider a situation in which a friend of mine points to a particular, distant hill and asks me whether I would like to join him in climbing it. Since I am somewhat tired, I answer that at present I do not feel like it. This negative reply is based on my actual or imagined experiences of a Euclidean movement of my body: if I agree to go, I will first have to walk the long (Euclidean) distance to the foot of the hill and then will have to climb the steep (Euclidean) path to its top. Clearly, even in "untouched nature" the human body constitutes, and is routinely employed as, a transportable Euclidean standard. Although Heelan (1983, 251) notices this use of the human figure, he appears to see it—wrongly, I think—as inconsequential to his general philosophical interpretation of space perception.

In sum, the significance of human action entailed by the method of profile variation appears to be denied by the theory of hyperbolic vision. This theory encounters problems when it is applied to situations that require an intrinsic coordination of instrumental actions, mutual communications, and perceptual claims. Therefore, if we want to explain the pertinence and success of perception in dealing with our material and social world, we need to take into account the full role of human action, over and above acknowledging the instrumentally embodied extension of human sense organs. The experienced perceiver is the one who is able to integrate the actually perceived profile with a sufficiently varied set of possible profiles. This integration requires not merely a pictorial but also an action perspective. These two perspectives constitute irreducible but interwoven dimensions of the way we routinely realize perceptual acts within our life world.

THE MATERIAL REALIZATION AND CONCEPTUAL

INTERPRETATION OF OBSERVATIONAL PROCESSES

I conclude part 1 of this book by presenting a general philosophical account of human observation. I do so on the basis of the results obtained in the preceding five chapters. That is to say, I both use (parts of) the views of the authors discussed and develop the critical points I have made in assessing these views. My account employs three basic notions: the notions of an observational process and its material realization and conceptual interpretation. Hence, the more specific objective of this chapter is to develop and clarify these notions and to vindicate the resulting account of human observation by discussing and refuting a number of possible counterarguments.

But first of all, there is a preliminary matter of terminology. In the previous chapters three different terms are employed: experience, perception, and observation. Clearly, these notions are closely related, and quite a few authors use them indiscriminately. Although not too much hinges upon it, in the present context I prefer the notion of observation. One reason is that this is a term that applies both to ordinary life and to scientific practice. Another reason is that the focus of this book is on vision, seeing, and the like, as conscious processes. Gaining experience, in contrast, may also involve interactions with the world through the other senses. Perception, finally, seems to carry the most narrow connotations of the three, at least in the context of philosophy. In many epistemological discussions, for example, perception is routinely opposed to cognition.

Thus let us stick to "observation." More specifically, my subject is the observation of external objects. In making observations of external objects we make essential use of our body. Hence the phenomenon of proprioception —the (nonvisual) experience of the position, orientation, and movement of (parts of) our own body—may play a role in observing external objects, but it is not itself the ultimate subject of my discussion.

Now consider the notion of an observational process. Using "observational process" as a fundamental notion means that an adequate philosophical theory of observation should go beyond an account of how our eyes or brains register the ultimate results of observational processes; at the same time, it should also go beyond a mere analysis of the content of those results. Important insights may be gained from studying the ways this content and these results emerge from a more comprehensive, spatiotemporally extended observational process. In Kantian terms, such a study should provide an extensive explication of the "conditions of the possibility" of human observation.

As we see in more detail below, studying observation from this perspective involves focusing both on the role of individual observers in realizing and interpreting observational processes and on the broader natural and sociocultural aspects of those processes. The natural and sociocultural contexts offer resources and include constraints that are drawn upon by individual observers in realizing and interpreting observational processes. Thus an exposition of the conditions of the possibility of human observation needs to address both its individual and its transindividual aspects.

This account of observational processes builds on the analyses in the preceding chapters. In outline, it agrees with Patrick Heelan's notion of an embodied act of perception, with its physical and cognitive moments and its embeddedness in a sociocultural World. A concrete example of a comprehensive observational process is provided in the seven-step reconstruction of Paul Churchland's account of the neural network observation of rocks and mines. My reconstruction of this process demonstrates more than the necessity of including a human observer. It also emphasizes the significance of the natural and sociocultural contexts and of the role of other human agents in realizing (parts of) this observational process.

A basic question that arises from focusing on observational processes concerns the relation between the process and its result. Much can be learned from seeing the content of an observation as resulting from a more comprehensive process. Yet endorsing this statement also involves a risk. The risk is to conceive of the meaning of this content as being completely determined by the process from which it results. Such a conception, however, would commit the genetic fallacy, that is to say, it would imply that the nature of a result is completely fixed by the nature of the process that has generated it.[1]

The focus here is on two further questions regarding the idea of an observational process. The first is how such a process can be conceptualized in more detail: which notions should be included in an adequate philosophical account of an observational process? The second question is how a particular observational process can be more precisely delineated: when and where does a specific process begin and end? My strategy in addressing these two questions is to answer the second on the basis of a resolution of the first.

The Material Realization of Observational Processes

We may fruitfully conceive of observational processes in terms of the two key notions of material realization and conceptual interpretation. As I will demonstrate, any observational process is always materially realized and conceptually interpreted right from the start.

Consider first the notion of material realization. In general terms, the meaning of this notion can be explained relatively easily. The term "material" denotes the strictly material aspects of an observational process, while the term "realization" refers to the activities of human agents who realize the observational process through action and intervention. Three important features of this notion of material realization need to be emphasized. First, material realization is not an act of creation (in the literal sense of this term) but rather an activity that exploits available natural potentialities and sociocultural resources (compare with Radder 1996, 76–80). Second, in general, other human agents apart from the individual observer will be involved, or will have been involved, in materially realizing the observational process. The example of the rock-mine observational process nicely illustrates this point. Third, it is crucial to bear in mind that the notions of material realization and conceptual interpretation do not stand for separable components or distinct stages of an observational process. These notions can only be analytically distinguished from such a process. Thus the phrase "material realization of an observational process" (or its "conceptual interpretation") should be read as a shorthand for the aspect of materially realizing (or conceptually interpreting) such a process.[2]

Several more specific notions that figure in my discussion of observation in the preceding chapters can be conveniently combined under the heading of material realization. Thus the material realization of observational processes involves the (material aspects of) the following types of actions and interventions.

1. Observing an object depends on actual, concomitant actions, such as pupil adjustments and eye movements, motion of body parts, or locomotion. As early as 1896, John Dewey stressed the importance of acting in his naturalistic theory of knowledge. "In a certain sense it is the movement which is primary, and the sensation which is secondary, the movement of body, head and eye muscles determining the quality of what is experienced" (quoted in Biesta 1992, 53).

But the notion of material realization goes beyond the idea of mere action by also highlighting what action brings, or is supposed to bring, about. That is to say, when the right conditions for observing an object are not yet present, they need to be materially realized by concomitant intervention. This material realization may involve a variety of interventions, such as cleaning our contact lenses, securing that there is enough light, removing interfering obstacles, preparing the object in a specific way, and so on. In the preceding chapters many examples are given of the role of such concomitant actions and interventions in the material realization of (various types of) observational processes. Some of those actions are carried out automatically (most of our eye movements), others have to be learned but are then performed routinely (securing sufficient light), and still others require, and continue to require, skilled practice and attention (observing a comet through a telescope, preparing a specimen of some tissue for microscopic observation).

2. Making observations depends not merely on concomitant human actions but also on past actions. When we "immediately" see a two-dimen-

sional picture as representing a three-dimensional bear climbing the other side of a tree, we apply internalized conceptual schemes that are generalized from preceding actions. It was Jean Piaget, in particular, who emphasized the significance of past action for structuring later observations (see Piaget 1972, especially chap. 4). In discussing the empirical content of scientific experiments, Peter Janich (1998, 109–10) similarly points out the importance of the action-theoretic distinction between actual actions and the action schemes that we have learned on the basis of preceding actions and that are employed in realizing concrete experimental processes.

Although I do not want to deny the important role of actual bodily action in the realization of observational processes, Piaget and Janich are right in emphasizing the significance of past action. Hence Yves Gingras correctly criticizes Andrew Pickering's exclusively actualist notion of agency on the basis of Piaget's more structuralist conception of action (see Pickering 1995b; Gingras 1997, 318–20). Furthermore, Piaget's point seems also to have been unjustly forgotten in some of the recent visual science accounts of perception (compare with Noë 2001).

3. In addition to presupposing past actions and employing concomitant actions, observation is also oriented toward possible or future actions. This idea of observation for action is stressed by Maurice Merleau-Ponty, who points out the correlation between the perceived world and the possibility of bodily action. "What counts for the orientation of the spectacle is not my body as it in fact is, as a thing in objective space, but as a system of possible actions, a virtual body with its phenomenal 'place' defined by its task and situation. My body is wherever there is something to be done" (quoted in Ihde 1990, 39).

The claim that observation is "for action" is supported by recent experimental results in the psychology of perception (see Noë 2001; O'Regan and Noë 2001a, 2001b; Looren de Jong, Bem, and Schouten 2004, 287–92; Van Eck, Looren de Jong, and Schouten 2006, 175–91). In the tradition of John Dewey and James Gibson, visual scientists have investigated the interconnectedness of vision and (future) action. Two important conclusions emerge from these investigations, one negative and one positive. First, human observers appear neither to record nor to construct detailed and all-encompassing visual representations of their environment. Second, people see whatever they need to see given their situation and the tasks at hand. For example, when we are thirsty we will keep seeing the pub we are approaching, but we will often fail to notice changes in our visual field (even if they are quite substantial) that are unrelated or irrelevant to our current aim of quenching our thirst. This so-called change blindness effect proves to be operative in a significant number of different situations.

Thus action and observation are related in a variety of ways, as many authors have pointed out.[3] In spite of this, it is also true that many authors still ignore the role of material realization in observation, as in the case of Bas van Fraassen, Norwood Hanson, Peter Kosso, and Paul Churchland. Not only does this oversight imply that these views are incomplete; as we have seen, it also entails that quite a few of the more specific claims of these authors are highly questionable.

In concluding this discussion of the material realization of observational processes, I would like to add three further remarks. First, there is an ontological issue. I use the notion of materiality in a broad, nonreductionist sense. Thus it is clearly wider than the idea of the physical, which is often taken to imply a restriction to the entities of physics. Moreover, emphasizing the significance of materiality is not the same as advocating materialism, in the sense of a reductionist ontological doctrine. After all, not only are actual observational processes materially realized, they are also conceptually interpreted and embedded in sociocultural contexts.

Furthermore, the view that action is an indispensable aspect of making observations fits in well with the more general theory of embodied cognition. In recent years, interest in this theory has strongly increased. In an extensive review of work on embodied cognition (EC), Michael Anderson summarizes the approach as follows. "Along with research in situated cognition, EC further suggests that intelligence lies less in the individual brain, and more in the dynamic interaction of brains [and, more generally, human bodies] with the wider world—including especially the social and cultural worlds which are so central to human cognition—and therefore suggests that fields like sociology and cultural studies can themselves be important resources for (and in some guises are part of) the cognitive sciences" (2003, 126). Yet, as we will see in the account of the nonlocality of the meaning of concepts in part 2, human cognition cannot be reduced to situated, embodied action.

Finally, the notion of realization can be connected in a natural way to the modal idea of the possibility of alternative realizations of the same concept by means of different observational processes. This is an important point, which I discuss in detail in part 2 of this book. There, I relate the meaning of a concept to the set of possible observational processes for the description of which the concept may be successfully employed.

The Conceptual Interpretation of Observational Processes

The conceptual interpretation of observational processes constitutes a further key notion of my philosophical account of observation. The basic claim is that all human observation requires a conceptual interpretation (or, alternatively, a conceptual structuring or organization) of the materially realized observational processes. Including conceptual interpretation as a distinct notion implies that I assume—in contrast to Paul Churchland, among others—that concepts cannot be reduced to material or physical entities.

A first argument in favor of the claim that all human observation is conceptually interpreted is based on psychological experiments and anthropological studies, some of which are mentioned in chapter 3. Thomas Kuhn has discussed these and similar findings and drawn the following, significant conclusion. "Among the few things that we know about it [that is, sensation] with assurance are: that very different stimuli can produce the same sensations; that the same stimulus can produce very different sensations; and, finally, that the route from stimulus to sensation is in part conditioned by education" (1970b, 193).[4]

In sum, the relation between stimulus and response is not one-to-one. What we see is not fully determined by our visual stimuli or their distal causes, and it depends on specific characteristics of the observers and the observational process. I take this to be a plausibility argument. It does not strictly prove the role of conceptual interpretation in observation, but it positively suggests the possibility of such a role.

Two other arguments are more direct. A second argument for the claim that observation requires conceptual interpretation draws on the fact that "to observe" is an achievement verb, in Gilbert Ryle's sense of that term. In this respect, observing agrees with our ordinary-life notion of seeing. Performing an act of observing or seeing entails achieving a result that must be circumscribed in one way or another. We can "just gaze" or "just stare" but we cannot "just observe" or "just see." We always observe or see, or fail to observe or see, something definite. Hence, in Hanson's terminology, all observing is always observing-as. The implication is that it is impossible to say, "I observed something but I have no idea whatsoever about the observed object or the materially realized observational process."

Heelan's rendering of Edmund Husserl's account of the outer and inner perceptual horizons nicely illustrates these points. From a purely physical point of view, the input of our eyes is a complex array of radiation. Hence, observing determinate, three-dimensional objects requires making further differentiations. Apparently, in observing a scene we implicitly construe certain parts of our visual field as foreground and other parts as background. In doing so, we conceptually carve out certain object profiles as our items of attention. Furthermore, we apparently construe these variable and temporary profiles as more or less bounded and relatively enduring three-dimensional objects. It is through our conceptual interpretation that we observe something like delimited and stable objects instead of a diffuse array of temporally variable and structurally limited physical inputs. Clearly, such interpretations are fallible. On closer inspection, some observable things (for instance, shadows or holographic projections) may prove not to be three-dimensional or enduring.

The third argument for the necessity of conceptual interpretation rests on the fact that observations can be correct, more or less correct, or incorrect. This requires a norm of success and hence a conceptual interpretation of what counts as success and whether or not it has been achieved in individual cases. As in the case of observational processes that include the operation of neural networks, this norm and this interpretation constitute an additional feature that cannot be derived from the physical systems themselves. More generally, materially realizing observational processes requires action and intervention. Yet not every action or intervention counts as successful. Hence claims of having made some specific observation through the relevant, materially realized process may be challenged and dismissed as being illusory.

By way of example, consider the following story. A lawsuit is being held, in which a priest appears as a witness. The priest claims to have seen the suspect at the relevant place and time. The defense, however, questions this testimony. The attorneys argue that the priest cannot possibly have seen their client, because (1) the light was dim, (2) the priest did not wear his glasses (as a matter of fact, of minus 2 diopters), and (3) he had used mind-altering substances. Thus, even if the priest really thinks and claims to have seen the suspect, this cannot have been the case because the correct conditions for this specific observation were not fulfilled.

The example demonstrates how the claim that an observation has been made may be challenged on the basis of its criteria of correctness. It also shows that the criteria for the correctness of observations and the question of whether or not they apply in the case at hand cannot be established simply on the basis of the laws of nature. That the light was really too dim might be objectively ascertainable, but it might just as well require a more or less subjective judgment. The relevance of wearing glasses is clearly a historical phenomenon. Before the invention of glass lenses, the eyesight of our priest might have counted as perfectly normal. Finally, in some cultures a priest's taking substances is part of his daily job and is even positively valued as a means to achieve enhanced vision.

It is important to be clear about what is not implied by the claim that human observation is conceptually interpreted. Here, I briefly mention three interconnected points, to which I come back in the next section. First, the fact that observation is always conceptually interpreted does not imply that all individual observers are always aware of all the interpretations they have and use. Second, this account of observation should not be read as saying that individual observers always elicit the conceptual interpretation through an explicit and conscious inference. Third, it is not assumed that conceptual interpretation always presupposes the ability to express the concepts linguistically.

I return to Abner Shimony's Kantian questions, which are mentioned in the discussion of theory ladenness in chapter 3. Shimony suggested that quite different sorts of interpreting concepts may be involved in observational processes. In particular, some of these concepts might be universally shared or even innate, while others might be variable or even under conscious control.

Shimony may well be right. After all, the above discussion shows that realizing observational processes requires a diversity of different concepts, varying from very general to quite specific. Yet answering Shimony's questions is not, or not primarily, a philosopher's task. The reason is that answering them requires extensive empirical research in, for instance, biology, psychology, historiography, and anthropology. Philosophy as such is simply not well equipped to answer such questions. Nevertheless, philosophy may exploit insights obtained in these special sciences to increase the plausibility of its claims about the scope of conceptual interpretations in structuring observational processes.

In this sense, I think that the following claims are plausible: observation, including the concepts that interpret it, has to be learned (e.g., seeing a three-dimensional object "in" the manifold of its profiles or seeing a comet); some of those interpreting concepts are shared by all human beings (e.g., the notion that, normally, observations are intentional, that is to say, they are about entities that are external to the entities that make up the sense organs or brain of the observer); some observations are interpreted by culturally specific concepts (e.g., seeing a cassowary bird or seeing an X-ray tube); sometimes, the content of an observation cannot be changed by means of a conscious decision (e.g., our perception of the Müller-Lyer illusion); but sometimes it can (e.g., switching from seeing an X-ray tube to seeing a manufactured configuration of glass, metal plates, wires, and the like). This differentiated view of the scope of conceptual interpretations has the additional advantage that it accounts for the possibility of novel observations in a natural way. After all, we may engage in new observational processes and along the way develop new interpreting concepts for these processes.

A significant philosophical conclusion from this discussion is that what we see is not uniquely and unambiguously determined by a presumably ready-made external reality. Thus I agree with this part of Hanson's account and disagree with Kosso's objectivist interpretation of the interaction-information account. Analogously, the explicit recognition of the fact that interpreting concepts may be culturally specific precludes a view in which the life world of a particular culture is being unreflectively interpreted as the foundation of allegedly certain or apodictic perceptual judgments. As we have seen in chapter 6, such a view crops up occasionally in Heelan's hermeneutics of perception. In my view, two people with (possibly radically) different conceptual interpretations may well be engaged in the same (or a similar) material realization of an observational process. But because "the same material realization" does not imply "the same (conceptually interpreted) observational content," they will not necessarily see the same thing.[5]

Furthermore, it is important not to confuse a conceptual interpretation with a mental copy. That is to say, the claim that all observation requires a conceptual interpretation does not imply that this interpretation somehow provides a complete and detailed mental representation of the entire visual field. The latter claim has been rightly criticized in recent studies of perceptual experience. This criticism, however, does not license the Gibsonian conclusion that observation is direct, in the sense that integrating concepts play no role at all. Consider the following quotation. "When we see, it perceptually seems to us as if we encounter a world of immense detail, but it doesn't seem to us as if we have all that environmental detail in our minds at once. . . . Rather, it seems to us as if the environment is there, and as if we can extract information from the environment by moving our eyes or head or by reorienting our bodies" (Noë 2001, 49).

If this account of experience and the active mind were to be read as implying that we can do without integrating concepts altogether, there would be no explanation for the "as ifs." That is to say, we require a conceptual interpretation to integrate the fragmentary visual inputs into an environment that is (permanently) there, and this interpretation is adequate when it proves to be a reliable guide to our further explorations of that environment.

Finally, the conceptual interpretation of observational processes is not the exclusive achievement of the individual observer. It is in particular the fact that observation has to be learned that requires the presence of a socio-cultural community.[6] This community is the source of conceptual interpretations and of the criteria for successful observation. Thus the primary locus of conceptual interpretations is the relevant sociocultural context rather than the individual observer. This entails that the philosophical claim that all observation is conceptually interpreted is itself a theoretical claim. It does not primarily denote a conscious act or assume an explicit inference on the part of individual observers. Yet implicit uses of conceptual interpretations can be made explicit, either in cases when those uses are contested or through reflexive analysis.

Countering Counterarguments

Several obvious questions and objections may be, and in fact have been, raised with respect to the view that observation always requires a conceptual interpretation. If this view is to be plausible, such questions and objections need a convincing reply.

A first important counterargument claims that direct, unmediated observation is possible. Quite a few authors still advocate this view. Remarkably enough, these authors hardly ever discuss, let alone take account of, the mediation that results from the material realization of observational processes. Instead, they focus on the conceptual interpretation and claim that there is a significant class of observations that does not require intervening concepts. Thus Robert Hudson starts a paper on this subject as follows. "My task in this paper is to defend the occurrence of what I call 'direct perception.' Direct perception is the process of perceiving an object without the mediation of concepts. As such, the object directly perceived is 'concept-less' or 'theory-free.' The claim that there is such a thing as direct perception in this sense has been much maligned since the post-positivist turn in the philosophy of science heralded in the writings of Kuhn, Hanson and Feyerabend" (2000, 357).

In a similar vein, René van Woudenberg (2000) argues against perceptual relativism, the claim that what we see is in some fundamental sense relative to a conceptual interpretation. While Hudson aims to support an empiricist philosophy, Van Woudenberg relies on commonsense arguments in the spirit of Thomas Reid. Their motivation is the same, however. They both try to vindicate the claim that perception is a source of unbiased knowledge of the way the world, in itself, is.

To that end, both Hudson and Van Woudenberg employ the distinction, introduced by Fred Dretske, between the perception of objects (or things) and the perception of facts. In an act of object-perception one observes an object *x* without being aware that it is *x* or has features *F*. In contrast, fact-perception means that one observes *x* and is aware that it is *x* and has features *F*. Dretske provides the following illustration. "The first time I became aware of an armadillo (I saw it on a Texas road), I did not know what it was. I did not even know what armadillos were, much less what they looked like. My ignorance did not impair my eyesight, of course. I saw the animal. I was aware of it ahead of me on the road" (1993, 266).

Thus the example is meant to show that we can object-perceive the armadillo without fact-perceiving that it is an armadillo. More generally, it is concluded that observing an object *x* does not necessarily presuppose the possession and use of the concept of *x*. With the help of this and similar distinctions and examples, Hudson and Van Woudenberg claim that direct or unmediated observation is possible and in fact occurs all the time.

The former conclusion—that we are able to see something without knowing what it is—seems to be undeniable. Yet I would phrase it somewhat more carefully as the claim that observer *A* may see an object without seeing that it is, according to observer *B* and others, an armadillo. (I prefer this formulation because it allows for genuine controversy about what it is that is being observed, as in the case of the observation of a whale, where *A* sees a fish when *B* sees a mammal). Formulated thus, I fully endorse this claim. In fact, the very rationale for distinguishing between the material realization and the conceptual interpretation of observational processes can be found in the situation in which the same material realization is differently interpreted by different observers (see Radder 1988, chap. 3). Moreover, Van Fraassen, Hanson, and Churchland, to mention some of the proponents of the theory ladenness of observation, would also find no problem in subscribing to the claim that we are able to see something without knowing what it is (according to other observers). However, to conclude that this claim implies the possibility of direct, unmediated observation is a non sequitur. The reason is straightforward. In observing the object, A may well have employed concepts other than the ones used by B. In the armadillo example, this is clearly the case. Apparently, Dretske fact-perceived that it was an animal and that it was ahead of him on the road. The situation is similar to the one encountered in Van Fraassen's example of observing a tennis ball, discussed in chapter 2. As I argue there, some observers may have failed to observe-that it was a tennis ball, because they observed-that it was a baseball.

The conclusion must be that this specific argument for direct, unmediated observation fails.[7] Consequently, a valid argument would have to provide other evidence for the possibility of conceptually unmediated observation, and it would have to refute the claims against this possibility discussed in the preceding section.

Finally, in discussing the role of concepts in observation we should be careful about what precisely is at issue. In individual observers, conceptual interpretations function as internalized schemes that can be applied to particular situations in a quasi-automatic manner. Hence the view that all observation is conceptually interpreted does not necessarily imply that each individual observer always has explicit beliefs about the observed object and always makes a conscious inference about the nature of what is being observed. In quite a few discussions of this issue, however, these distinctions are blurred. Thus one often encounters unnoticed shifts from the view that observation requires the application of concepts to the views that it entails having explicit beliefs and making conscious inferences. My account of observation demands that the role of conceptual interpretation should be carefully distinguished from that of explicit beliefs and conscious inferences.

A second counterargument to the claim that observation is conceptually interpreted is also quite common (compare with Dretske 1993, 268). It runs as follows. Infants and animals do not possess concepts, yet they surely observe things; hence it cannot be true that all observation involves conceptual interpretation. Before responding to this objection, we should be clear about what precisely is being questioned. At issue is not simply whether infants or animals see, but whether they observe in the same way as (mature) humans do.

In the case of infants, the counterargument fails because of the implausibility of its first premise. As psychological research has shown, infants can be said to possess concepts at a remarkably young age, and certainly before they are able to express these concepts linguistically.[8] Given the possibility of materially realizing observational processes, the perceptual capacities of infants develop concurrently with their mastery of the relevant organizing concepts (see also Koningsveld 1973, 12–13). For this reason, Hanson's claim that the observations of infants are "indeterminate" is also incorrect, as is the mixing up of conceptual and linguistic interpretation by Hanson and Heelan. Human infants conceptually structure their observations long before they are able to tell you what they see. Thus we need to distinguish between a conceptual interpretation, which is generally required for human observation, and a linguistic expression of this interpretation, which may not always be available.

The case of animals is obviously different from that of infants. Their sense organs and bodies differ from ours to a smaller or larger extent. Moreover, finding out whether or not they possess and use concepts is difficult. Although a few recent studies of animal behavior claim that at least some primates have concepts, the issue remains controversial (see Stephan 1999). Hence my response to this counterargument is as follows: If animals possess concepts, they might be able to see as we do; if not, their experiences must be basically different from ours. Yet even if the latter were true, it would not constitute a reason to reject the theory that all human observation is conceptually interpreted. After all, as we have seen in this and the preceding chapters, this theory is supported by a great number and a large variety of human observational processes, whereas alternative theories have proved to be inadequate.

How to Delineate an Observational Process

Above I provide and vindicate a philosophical account of observational processes in terms of the notions of material realization and conceptual interpretation. What remains to be discussed is the issue of a more precise delineation of particular observational processes. What exactly should be included in an adequate philosophical account of a particular observational process? When and where does this specific process begin and end?

Conceptually interpreting observational processes entails, in Hanson's terminology, that we always observe something "as x." Now, I assume that all those features F_i of a particular observational process should be included in our account if, without the presence of F_i, we would observe x' instead of x. In addition, there may be further relevant conditions C_i, in the sense that, unless C_i is present, we are not able to observe anything at all. Of course, not all conditions of the type C will be equally interesting from a philosophical point of view.

By way of illustration, consider again the observation of a bear climbing up the other side of a tree. In this case, the above analysis implies that the feature "past locomotion of the observer" should be included in an adequate philosophical account of the observational process of seeing the figure as a bear climbing up the other side of a tree. Furthermore, "having eyesight" and "the presence of oxygen" are two conditions that are necessary for being able to make this observation at all. In this example, the first condition appears to be more interesting for a philosophy of human observation than the second. Yet there is no generally valid rule for deciding which of the C_i's constitute the philosophically interesting conditions. The main reason is that the acceptability of a proposed rule will be strongly dependent on the chosen metaphilosophical perspective. Thus, from his view of philosophy as conceptual analysis, Hanson concluded that "having eyesight" is not particularly interesting. Clearly, proponents of naturalistic theories of observation will disagree with this conclusion.

As a second example of how to delineate observational processes, consider the discussion of the observation of rock and mine sonar echoes with the help of a connectionist network. Again, we should include at least all those features F_i of the overall situation that make a specific difference with respect to the result of the observational process. Looking at the seven-step account of the rock-mine case presented in chapter 5, it will be clear that almost all the features of this analysis make such differences and hence are of the type F.[9] Thus these features should be taken into account in a comprehensive philosophical analysis of the rock-mine observational process.

Human Observers and Scientific Instruments

The theory of observation developed here agrees with those studies of scientific practice that take account of the overall observational or experimental processes and their material and conceptual dimensions (see, for example, Pinch 1985; Gooding 1990; Radder 1996, chap. 2). But the theory also applies to observations in everyday life. This may be made more intelligible by conceiving of a human observer as being analogous to an instrument as it is used in the practice of experimental science (thus following Kosso's information-interaction account in this respect). More precisely, a human observer may be seen to be a "self-interpreting observational instrument, which has been brought about in the course of a material and sociocultural evolution and which actively engages the world in attempts at materially realizing and conceptually interpreting observational processes." Several aspects of this analogy are worth a brief explanation.

First of all, the human visual apparatus may be, and often is, corrected or enhanced, for instance, through glasses, contact lenses, surgical interventions, binoculars, or microscopes. This fact fits naturally within an instrumental conception of human observers. Moreover, just like a laboratory instrument, such a corrected or enhanced human instrument needs to meet specific operating and maintenance conditions to function well. Furthermore, in using instruments in experimental practice, we engage the world and are sensitive to its opportunities and resistances. This engagement requires certain skills, which are sometimes widely shared and routinely applied and sometimes more specific and rare. As I show in this and the previous chapters, these aspects of the use of scientific instruments are also characteristic of the realization of observational processes.

Second, the distinction between the material realization and the conceptual interpretation of the functioning and use of scientific instruments can also be fruitfully applied to human observational processes. Thus the notion of material realization allows for different human agents who realize different parts of the observational process. In science, an observation by a particular observer will usually involve a variety of instruments realized (in the sense of constructed, tested, and operated) by other human agents. For instance, a particular act of observing solar neutrinos requires the realization of an elaborate observational process in which a variety of other people are involved (see Pinch 1985). The same is true of processes of contact lens observation. Here, too, a variety of other people are involved in realizing the observational process (in the sense of manufacturing, testing, selling, and maintaining the lenses).

Third, the distinction between realization and interpretation takes account of the possibility of different conceptual interpretations of the same material realization. As in experimentation, in observation the same realizations may be differently interpreted: as a tennis ball or a baseball, as an armadillo or a weird animal, as an X-ray tube or a device made of glass, metal, and wires, to mention a few examples.

Finally, focusing on the instrumental nature of human observation draws attention to the species relativity of observation. The "observational instruments" of unaided human observers differ from those of animals, such as bees, bats, or bonobos. Hence human and animal observational processes may be expected to be more or less different. This fact should make us wary of making hasty extrapolations from animal experience to human experience. In addition, smell often plays a much more prominent role in the case of animals than it does in the case of humans. This fact also suggests that the visual part of animal experience may not be simply comparable to the visual component of human experience.

Thus the analogy with scientific instruments and their uses illuminates several important aspects of human observation. Yet it remains an analogy, which should not be taken for an identity. A human observer is not identical to a material instrument. For one thing, human observation is not a matter of a mere registration of causal effects; it essentially depends on intentional action. Moreover, human observers, unlike scientific instruments, are self-interpreting. They possess concepts and employ these in interpreting the materially realized observational process.

How a Subject Observes an Object or Fact

Extending from my explanation of the meaning and scope of observational processes and of the analogy between human observers and scientific instruments, I can provide a summarizing account of what it means for an individual observer to observe the object x or the fact that x is P. Subject S observes the object x (or the fact that x is P), if a correct material realization and conceptual interpretation of an observational process has resulted in a presentation of x (or of x is P) that is noticed as such by S.

Three notions from this definition require additional explanation. The qualification "as such" means that S's noticing implies the implicit or explicit employment of the relevant conceptual interpretation. This guarantees that S sees the object or fact under the relevant conceptual interpretation. The requirement of "correctness" takes account of the fact that observations may be correct or incorrect. In this and the previous chapters, the (in)correctness of material realizations and conceptual interpretations is repeatedly discussed and exemplified. However, since my focus is not on epistemological issues, providing a systematic account of the notion of observational correctness is clearly beyond the scope of this book.

Furthermore, there is the notion of a "presentation." A presentation may be an image of x, but it may also be a more general mark of the presence of x. An image will result in the case of S's noticing of x by means of a naked eye, a contact lens, a telescope, an MRI or PET scanner, an optical or electron microscope, or any other instrument from the increasing host of modern imaging technologies. Such "primary" instruments allow us to observe chairs, the moons of Jupiter, brain tumors, plant cells, DNA molecules, and the like. A more general mark will be presented in the case of S's noticing of x by means of a clock, a thermometer, a cloud chamber, a neutrino detector, or any other instrument of this type. These "secondary" instruments allow us to observe times, temperatures, atoms, neutrinos, and the like.[10]

Finally, an important assumption underlying this account of how an individual subject may observe an object or fact can be stated succinctly as follows. If human observation is always and necessarily instrumentally mediated through our specific sensory apparatus, its nature will not change if additional instruments are introduced and used in realizing observational processes.[11] Hence ordinary observation using few or no artificial instruments proves to be continuous with scientific observation, which may make extensive use of a great variety of instruments.

HOW CONCEPTS STRUCTURE THE WORLD

In part 1, I analyze scientific and ordinary observation in terms of the material realization and conceptual interpretation of observational processes. I present many examples and several accounts of how making observations depends on material realization and conceptual interpretation. Part 2 revisits the relationship between materially realized observational processes and conceptual interpretations, but it focuses on different philosophical issues. Its primary subject is how concepts, which have been or might be used in interpreting materially realized observational processes, relate to the world. As in part 1, the account is meant to apply both to everyday and to scientific concepts. My aim is to show that concepts both structure the world and abstract from it. The Kantian claim—that concepts structure the world—is explained and discussed, rather briefly, in this chapter. The following chapters, then, address the main claim of this second part of the book, namely, that concepts abstract from the world.

My investigation builds on the analysis of the role of concepts in materially realizing observational processes. Consequently, it bears upon those concepts that are supposed to say something about the world and not upon purely fictitious or exclusively formal concepts. The term "world" is used here in the sense of the world "in as far as it is accessible through realizing and interpreting observational processes." This is similar to the so-called phenomenal world, but my use of this phrase is much broader than that which Immanuel Kant or Bas van Fraassen had in mind. Indeed, in the view of observation proposed in part 1, all entities denoted by means of conceptually interpreted observational processes belong to the phenomenal world. It should also be clear that this phenomenal world does not coincide with the human-independent reality. The question of what observational processes may teach us about a human-independent reality, however, is beyond the scope of this book (see Radder 1988 for a discussion of this question in the context of scientific realism).

Concepts as Methods of Observation

Herman Koningsveld (1973, 1976) has developed an interesting and detailed theory of the meaning of (empirical) concepts by analyzing their role in making observations. First, he addresses the issue of how new concepts may be formed in the course of observing a class of unknown entities. His central claim is that empirical concepts essentially are, or entail, a method of observation. Forming a concept and learning how to see the entities as instantiations of it are two sides of the same coin. "Concept formation means precisely this learning to observe in the appropriate way. And therefore: the empirical concept formed entails a method of observation. . . . Once one has learned to observe as one should, one has formed concepts. This 'as one should,' this appropriateness, constitutes the meaning of the concepts" (Koningsveld 1973, 11, emphasis omitted).

More specifically, when we have acquired a certain concept, we know, first, the kind of entities to which the concept applies (its domain) and, second, which factors are relevant or irrelevant in correctly applying the concept to an observational situation. In Koningsveld's view, these domain specifiers and factors of (ir)relevancy constitute two central elements of the meaning of a concept. A concept includes particular domain specifiers and factors of (ir)relevancy because it is always connected to other concepts. Thus part of the meaning of the ordinary color concept of "being red" is that it cannot be applied to a sound and that the flavor of an object is irrelevant to its being red. Hence an individual concept is not an isolated entity since it is always related to a network of other concepts. Its meaning derives, in part, from the number and nature of its connections with other concepts.[1]

Koningsveld concludes that concepts produce or increase order in initially less well-structured observational situations and, more generally, that the world—in as far it is knowable through making observations—is a conceptually structured world. In this respect, he clearly belongs to the Kantian tradition (see Koningsveld 1976, 133-34). In contrast to Kant's method, the way these conclusions are reached is more empirical. From cases that show how concepts increase order in an initially less well-structured situation and from the claim that these cases are representative of all concepts, it is concluded that the world—in as far as it can be empirically accessed—is a conceptually structured world.

In developing these views, Koningsveld proposes and discusses a certain experimental setup for studying processes in which new concepts are being learned. He starts with presenting a number of figures, printed on a sheet of paper (see figure 8.1). Next, he claims that these figures can be classified into three subsets, corresponding to three different concepts (I, II, and III). The task for the learner is to acquire these concepts in a process of trial and error. Koningsveld himself plays the role of the teacher who—in this experimental setup—fully understands the ins and outs of these concepts. The learning process develops through particular trials by the student ("this entity has property I") and assessments by the teacher (wrong). At times, a student proposes a certain general trial, which proves to be an error (for in-

FIGURE 8.1. Items to be conceptualized. Reproduced from Koningsveld (1976, 127).

stance, I = Greek characters, II = Roman characters, and III = logical and mathematical symbols). The learning process ends when the learner, sooner or later, has obtained full competence in classifying the entities. This competence shows itself when routinely continued use of the concepts by the learner is judged to be correct by the teacher (see figure 8.2).

I will name the three new concepts *thob* (I = figures with both straight and curved line segments), *urve* (II = only curved line segments), and *raig* (III = only straight line segments). Koningsveld used to perform this experiment in his classes with his students. In these experiments, the above results were confirmed.[2] In Dutch, Koningsveld's names of the three terms (*bied, mork,* and *get*) provide a clue as to the sense of the concepts, although they are strictly speaking meaningless. In my English rendering I have retained this feature of the experiment.

The experiment starts from a fixed domain of entities, namely, a set of figures printed on a sheet of paper. Moreover, the experimental setup assumes the existence of three concepts and three corresponding subsets. In the course of the process the learner acquires the concepts and, in doing so, discovers what is relevant (geometrical form) and what is not (for example, being a logical symbol). Not every factor that is relevant needs to come up in each particular run of the experiment. For instance, incidentally students might spill water on the sheets, with the effect that they become curly, or they might think it useful to examine the figures through a strong magnifying glass. It is likely that the experiment will not work in these cases. It may be only then that the teacher realizes that flatness of the sheets and looking with the naked eye is required for a successful performance of the experiment.

The experiment confirms the claim—which is also endorsed by most proponents of connectionism—that observation has to be learned. Making observations is not a matter of merely opening one's eyes. According to Koningsveld (1976, 131–35), to acquire a concept is to learn to observe in a specific way. He concludes that a concept is, primarily, a method of observation, which marks out a domain of application and which implies several (possibly partially unknown) conditions of relevancy and irrelevancy. Clearly, the concepts of thob, urve, and raig define a domain of entities and

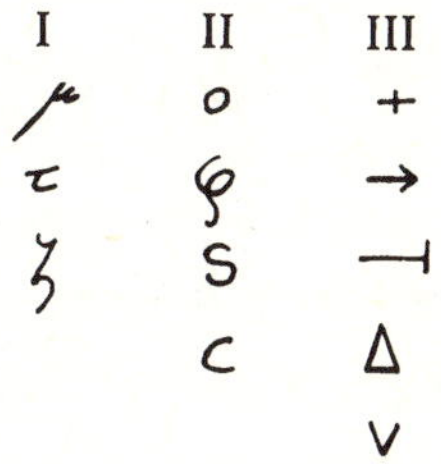

FIGURE 8.2. The thob-urve-raig conceptualization. Reproduced from Koningsveld (1976, 129).

structure it in a specific way. There are, however, alternative ways to structure this domain. After all, in a different context the rejected conjecture of Greek, Roman, and logical-mathematical characters might have been counted as correct.

One might object that this thob-urve-raig experiment is not representative of all processes of concept formation, for two reasons. First, in this specific setup the concepts to be learned can be defined and used on the basis of a simple and explicit rule. This aspect of the experiment, however, merely serves a pedagogical function, and it does not detract from the philosophically relevant conclusions that are drawn from the experiment. Second, the thob-urve-raig experiment starts from a situation in which the teacher has already acquired the relevant concepts, and hence it might be considered not representative in this respect. Yet Koningsveld may convincingly argue that the philosophically relevant features of his account also apply to the formation of genuinely novel concepts (which does not, of course, mean that this account covers anything that might be said about the development of novel concepts).

Suppose that no teacher is present in the thob-urve-raig experiment and that the students try to classify the entities by themselves. The difference, then, is that they themselves have to decide on what, ultimately, counts as the correct classification of the entities in question. During this process they will draw on resources and anticipate expectations from the epistemic, linguistic, and sociocultural communities to which they belong. Surely, it is not certain that they will come up with the thob-urve-raig classification. Perhaps they will classify the entities in terms of Greek and Roman characters and logical-mathematical symbols. But they might also settle on a five-fold categorization or might even conclude that these entities are unclassifiable. Thus without a teacher being present the concrete observational process and its result may well be different. This fact as such, however, does not provide a sufficient reason to doubt the general philosophical conclusions Koningsveld draws from his thob-urve-raig experiment.

THE EXTENSIBILITY OF CONCEPTS TO NOVEL OBSERVATIONAL PROCESSES

Herman Koningsveld argues that concepts structure the world, a big philosophical claim about which much more could be, and has been, said. I think that, ultimately, Koningsveld's Kantian claim is convincing. To conclude, however, that the full meaning of concepts can be explained on the basis of an analysis of particular processes in which those concepts have been learned is another matter. Yet this is Koningsveld's view, since he claims that the meaning of concepts is constituted by the appropriate method of observing the entities denoted by these concepts (1973, 11). In contrast, I argue that concepts not only structure the world but also abstract from it. This specific kind of abstraction plays a decisive role when we intend to use concepts in realizing novel observational processes. Taking account of abstraction leads to a different philosophical interpretation of the meaning of concepts and their relationship to the world.[1]

First, we need to be a little more explicit about the kind of concepts that are at issue. Since the focus is on the extensibility of concepts to novel domains in the world, my discussion does not apply to those concepts for which this notion does not make sense. Thus concepts expressed by individual terms, such as the concept of "Amsterdam" or the concept of "the sun," are excluded from consideration. The same holds for concepts expressing logical connectives, such as "not" or "and." Apart from these, however, the account is meant to apply to a variety of different kinds of concepts: both concepts referring to things (e.g., birds) and concepts referring to properties (e.g., being feathered), both concepts of "empirical" entities (e.g., tree) and of "theoretical" entities (e.g., atom), and both concepts denoting natural objects (e.g., stars) and artificial objects (e.g., shoes).

To explain and support the claim that such concepts abstract from the world, I propose a possible replication of the thob-urve-raig experiment. After all, the particular experiment performed and discussed by Koningsveld need not be the end of the story. Let us imagine that the three new concepts, thob, urve, and raig, have become entrenched in our culture (as they were in Koningsveld's classes) and that someone attempts to teach them to a number of blind people. This plan requires a new experimental setup, for example, of the following kind. The new teacher has the pictured geometric forms manufactured in various sizes and from different tangible materials. He or she puts them in a box and asks the blind people to examine them by touch and to arrange them into three categories by distributing them over three different boxes. A learning process analogous to the one in the first experiment may unfold. Some possible conjectures (I = large, II = intermediate, and III = small, or I = soft, II = in-between, and III = hard) will be failures, but after some time the blind pupils will, presumably, have learned the concepts in question.

Of course, one might further analyze this process by focusing on what is learned by the blind pupils through their interaction with the teacher and the empirical situation. In this case, the second experiment proves to be entirely analogous to the first one, and no new theoretical insights may be expected. It is also possible, though, to look at the two experiments from a different perspective. Let us position ourselves at the moment when the first experiment has been successfully completed, whereas the second one has been proposed and accepted as being sensible but has not yet been performed. Thus at this moment the second experiment is an intended experiment (but not, in the sense in which this term is often used in philosophy of science, a thought experiment). On the one hand, we have acquired the concepts of thob, urve, and raig through a particular setup, or, in my terminology, a particular observational process. On the other hand, by agreeing that performing the second experiment is a sensible project we assume that these concepts might also be applied to a different observational process. Clearly, the two processes are substantially different, since almost all particular features of Koningsveld's experiment are irrelevant to its intended replication.

To analyze this practice of extending concepts by means of observations in new domains more generally, I make use of my account of observation as the material realization and conceptual interpretation of observational processes. For the sake of brevity, I also use the phrase "realizing the process" as a shorthand for "materially realizing the observational process under a specific conceptual interpretation." Making observations (e.g., of a thob figure) is not a matter of a passive reception of stimuli but essentially involves the material realization and conceptual interpretation of a comprehensive observational process. Some parts of this process have to be realized and interpreted on the spot by the individual observers and their social communities; other parts will be found as the sediment of preceding, long-term processes of material and sociocultural evolution.

In the case of Koningsveld's experiment, a descriptive account of its material realization might mention, among other things, a room with a number of people present and various sheets of paper containing sets of unknown figures, as well as the entire process of people inspecting the sheets, moving them around, making notes, talking to each other, and so on.[2] The (linguistic expression of the) conceptual interpretation of this process tells us that there are students and a teacher in a classroom, that they are involved in a process of learning to classify the weirdly shaped figures into three mutually exclusive classes, and that successfully realizing this process means that students' use of the notions of thob, urve, and raig is judged to be consistently right (by the teacher and, eventually, by the students themselves).

To interpret the proposed experiment with the blind students we need to make a further distinction. We designate one part or aspect of the overall conceptual interpretation of the observational process as its result. Thus defined, the conceptual interpretation of an observational process includes its result, and this result is always a conceptually interpreted result. Which part of the observational process is designated as its result will depend on the context. Setting apart a result enables us to focus on a specific part or aspect of the overall observational process and then consider this item regardless of the process from which it resulted. Generally speaking, results will be statements about some outcome of observational processes. An illustration is "this figure o is urve." Thus the result of an observational process is phrased with the help of concepts, but it is not itself a concept. In the case of a successful performance of Koningsveld's experiment, the result of the observational process comprises a sufficient number of correct statements about thob, urve, and raig entities by the students. This outcome is contingent in the sense that it might well turn out that some, or even all, of the students fail to acquire the concepts in question.

When we compare the second experiment, involving the blind people, to the first, we find that their material realization and conceptual interpretation differ in several respects. Hence the two observational processes should be expected to be quite different. In the first experiment, the eyesight of the students is a crucial aspect of the observational process. Moreover, in realizing this process, spilling water on the sheets should be avoided. In the second experiment, we do not have sheets with unknown visible figures but tangible forms of various materials and sizes. Here, the envisioned learning process needs to be based on capabilities of classifying the forms by means of touch and feel. Spilling water does not matter but twisting the material forms (in as far as they are flexible) does.

Yet the two experiments are not completely different because both aim at teaching a group of people to make correct observations and classifications of thob, urve, and raig things. Thus these two experiments share the same result. Note that this is a conceptually interpreted result. In terms of material realization the outcomes differ considerably. In the first experiment, we end up with paper sheets with three lists of written figures. In the case of the second experiment, we have a configuration of three boxes, each containing a part of the tangible, material forms.

Extensible Concepts and Their Nonlocal Meaning

In my philosophical account of this intended replication of the thob-urve-raig experiment I try to make sense of the future-oriented beliefs and actions of the people involved. This means that, under certain conditions, I am prepared to draw philosophical conclusions from plans and planned actions. In planning and designing the replication we apparently assume that the concepts of thob, urve, and raig might be realized in this case as well. That is to say, we suppose that these concepts remain meaningful in abstraction of the specific realization conditions of the first experiment. The sensible attempt to enlarge the scope of a concept by applying it to a materially different domain, including its novel relevance and irrelevance conditions, involves abstracting from the original realization context. I call a concept extensible if it has been successfully applied to a certain domain and if it might be used in one or more new domains. Thus a clear distinction is implied between the actual extension of a concept and its extensibility, its possible extension. The notion of an extensible concept is a modal notion in that it points to some set of realizability conditions that would enable its future extension if they could be and were to be concretely realized in actual space and time.

There is an obvious question that needs to be answered about extensible concepts thus defined: are not all concepts that have proved to be applicable to one domain, extensible to one or more other domains? This question requires a qualified response. On the one hand, being extensible in some direction seems to be an important characteristic of the kind of concepts we are addressing. After all, is it not the point of such concepts to be useful in various and varying domains? Given the variety and variability of our world, thinking and communicating would be difficult, if not impossible, if we always needed a new concept for each new domain of phenomena. On the other hand, concepts are not simply extensible in any arbitrary direction. Both practically and philosophically speaking, the realizability of observational processes cannot be taken for granted. In advance of any attempted extension it remains fully contingent whether or not, in actual practice, a concept can and will be successfully extended to a specific new domain. Here, "being contingent" is used in its common philosophical meaning of not being (logically or physically) necessary, rather than in its common sense meaning of being accidental or arbitrary.

Thus the notion of possible extension refers to de facto extensibility in the material and social world. Consider again our planned second experiment. In this case, it might well be that it proves to be impossible (in a certain period or perhaps forever) to manufacture the required material forms in such a way that they are appropriate for the experiment to succeed. Or there might be a lasting and effective taboo on subjecting disabled, blind people to experiments such as the one proposed. Or it might turn out that, for one reason or another, the blind students never really master the concepts in question. Yet, as a matter of fact, in many cases—both in everyday life and in science—the possibility of extension has proved to be real. Thus, although there is no hard-and-fast criterion for the correctness of extensibility claims—as Rainer Lange (1999, 31) seems to require—such claims can be empirically supported, thus making the extensibility of a concept more than a mere definition or posit.

The proposed account of extensible concepts and their contingent extensions can be summarized as follows. One component of the meaning of concepts derives from the way they structure particular observational processes through domain specifiers and through the implied conditions of what is relevant and what is irrelevant in realizing such processes. In addition, however, extensible concepts possess a nonlocal meaning, which transcends the meaning they have as interpretations of the results of the observational processes that have been realized so far.[3] Thus we may say that extensible concepts possess both a structuring and an abstracting meaning component. Although I think that these two components capture central aspects of the meaning of concepts, I do not claim that they exhaust their meaning. Concepts may have additional connotations, metaphorical senses, and the like. Because of these further aspects, I prefer to speak of concepts as having meanings, or, better still, meaning components, instead of concepts as being meanings.

More generally, one may distinguish three approaches to the problem of the meaning of concepts (Stokhof 2000; Gurova 2003). Most cognitive scientists define a concept as some kind of mental representation, and accordingly they claim that the meaning of a concept derives from the structure and function of this representation. In contrast, many linguists and linguistically oriented philosophers claim that the meaning of a concept is given by a definition, for instance, in terms of a set of individually necessary and jointly sufficient conditions or by means of a theoretical stipulation. Realist philosophers and logicians, finally, often emphasize that the meaning of a concept should be fixed by the relation between the concept and the world, for instance, by a nonlinguistic extension or reference.

My general view is that none of the three separate approaches can provide an adequate explanation of concepts and their meaning.[4] Hence a full theory of the meaning of concepts should take into account all three sources of meaning (mind, language, and world). My aim here, however, is much more limited. Clearly, the focus of the account of (extensible) concepts is on the relation between concepts and the world. Its aim is to explain central aspects of this relation, primarily in terms of an abstracting meaning component and more briefly in terms of a structuring meaning component.

One important feature of the philosophical theory of the meaning of (extensible) concepts is the assumption of nondeterminism. As we have seen, in the present context contingency means that it has not been determined in advance whether or not a concept, in our actual future world, can or will be extended through the realization of specific, novel observational processes. This is a rather weak and plausible assumption.[5] It is, for example, compatible with a nondeterminism due to a fundamental quantum-mechanical indeterminism, or to a basic human freedom, or to both.

Another notable feature of extensible concepts is that they do not have a fixed extension, in the classical sense of a set of objects to which they apply and which is fixed either by an objective reality or by a transcendental subject. Neither nature nor mind is capable of fixing the extension of our concepts. Clearly, this feature is also a consequence of the facts that, first, observational processes are not "given" but have to be materially realized in the world and, second, that it remains essentially contingent whether or not such processes can or will be realized in the future. Thus the claim that the meaning of extensible concepts is nonlocal contrasts with the causal theory of meaning. The latter theory does assume that the extension of general concepts is fixed, to wit, by the existence of natural kinds.[6] Moreover, in my account, all concepts lack a fixed extension. Hence this lack has nothing to do with the existence of "borderline cases" and a corresponding "fuzziness" of certain concepts, nor with a deficiency of knowledge on the part of the "average speaker" (compare with Putnam 1975, 217, 228–29).

A final characteristic of this account of the meaning of concepts bears upon the issue of their identity (compare with Rey 1994). In a formal sense, we may say that two concepts are identical if they have the same meaning. We may extend this to a partial identity for concepts that share one or more, but not all, of their meaning components. Thus two concepts that apply to the same domains and structure these domains in the same manner share their structuring meaning components, and hence they are identical in this respect. Clearly, this implies that the criteria for identity of the concept cannot be separated from the criteria of its application. Again, this is a straightforward consequence of the fact that part of the structuring meaning component of a concept derives from its use in observational processes.[7] As to the abstracting meaning components, we may say that two concepts would share these components if all their potential extensions were to coincide fully. Clearly, even if it is possible to define the identity of the abstracting meaning components in this formal manner, the assumption of nondeterminism implies that we can never know whether two concepts are identical in this respect.

For this reason, the related question of when different people have the same concepts can only be answered for the case of the structuring meaning component. In line with the discussion in this and the previous chapter, my answer to this question derives from the Wittgensteinian tradition: consistently similar use of the concept is all we have to support the claim that different people have the same concept. It goes without saying that, in practice, such claims will always be highly fallible.

EXTENSIBLE CONCEPTS, ABSTRACTION, AND NONLOCALS

Concepts both structure the world and abstract from it. Concepts structure the world because they specify one or more particular domains of application and a particular set of conditions of (ir)relevancy. Consequently, any successful extension of the concept to a substantially novel domain will lead to a (smaller or larger) shift in its structuring meaning component. The meaning of the concept of a mammal, to mention a familiar example, changed slightly when it was extended to the new domain of the whales. And the meaning of the concepts of thob, urve, and raig will change if a successful performance of the experiment with the blind pupils proves to be possible. After all, in that case thob, urve, and raig things can not only be seen but also be touched and felt. Thus explaining part of the meaning of a concept on the basis of how it structures different domains of experience runs counter to the doctrine that concepts (should) retain a fixed and invariable meaning in the course of time.[1] In addition, however, concepts also abstract from these particular domains and their conditions of (ir)relevancy in the process of being extended to new realization contexts. This implies that Herman Koningsveld's view of (empirical) concepts as particular methods of observation covers only one part of their function.

Abstraction as Leaving Out and Setting Apart

The aim of this chapter is to explain and develop the notion of abstraction that is implied in the intended extension of concepts. Both in ordinary language and in philosophical discourse abstraction has several meanings and entails various connotations. Discussing these meanings and connotations helps to clarify the specific notion of abstraction that is being proposed. I start with considering ordinary (English) language and, more particularly, the verb "to abstract." There seem to be three basic meanings involved: to abstract as leaving out, as setting apart, and as summarizing. To abstract in the sense of to summarize may be typical of English. This sense is not shared, for example, by the Dutch verb *abstraheren*. Yet it is important to take the idea of summarizing into account because it and its cognates play a significant role in philosophical discourse. Next, we have the adjective "abstract." This is often taken to be equivalent to "conceptual" or "theoretical," and it is generally opposed to "concrete." Finally, there is the noun "abstraction," which may refer either to the act of abstracting or to the state of being abstracted.

In the history of philosophy, notions of abstraction and abstractness have been employed in different branches of philosophy, and they have been applied to develop and vindicate various philosophical positions (see Blokhuis 1985). In contemporary debates, the notion of abstraction plays a less prominent role, but it is often implicitly presupposed. For instance, a generally taken-for-granted procedure of formal logic and formal semantics is to leave out all the particularities of a sentence—its expression and usage at a specific moment, in a specific language, by a specific speaker or writer, and by means of specific material signs—so as to focus on its pure "content." The result of this process is, it is assumed, the proposition that is being asserted through the specific act of uttering the sentence. Such propositions, then, are taken to be composed of concepts, in the same way as words are the building blocks of sentences. In such processes of abstraction the proposition and its constituent concepts are set apart by separating them, mentally but also graphically, from their linguistic, social, and physical manifestation in an actually uttered sentence.

In the theory of knowledge, to mention another branch of philosophy, a much-discussed question is whether or not general concepts and laws are (or can be) acquired by abstracting from the irrelevant features of a sufficient number of particular instances or states of affairs. In other words, are concepts and laws obtained by some procedure of summarizing the relevant features of the particular cases? Another issue in the theory of knowledge bears upon the epistemological status of abstract theories, as compared to that of concrete or direct empirical statements. Finally, in ontology the nature and existence of putative abstractions or abstract entities (such as universals, numbers, laws of nature, minds) have been debated extensively. In these debates the contrast with concrete entities, and their presumed philosophical virtues, plays a crucial role.

To examine the idea of extensible concepts and the implied notion of abstraction, consider a first observational process, the result of which is being interpreted in terms of a certain concept (for instance, the concept of *thob*). If this concept is extensible, it remains meaningful in abstraction from the particularities of the original observational process. Thus it has a meaning that transcends the meaning of the original realization context. Hence a first major aspect of this notion of abstraction—used here as the act or process of abstracting—is the idea of leaving out. But it is a leaving out in a specific sense (which is of course expedient, since the idea of leaving out as such is too vague to be helpful). The notion of abstraction that is at issue here applies to the procedure of extending concepts through their intended use in the realization of genuinely novel observational processes. In this context, abstraction means that we leave out from the conceptual interpretation of the original process everything but its result. And we do so with a view to a potential extension of the concept through realizing a novel observational process. When the original and the envisioned observational processes are radically different, we leave out everything but the result of the first process. In the event that the two processes differ less, we abstract from a part of the original process.

Next, consider abstracting in the sense of setting apart. In one way or another, some idea of setting apart plays a role in almost all theories of abstraction that have been proposed in the history of philosophy. The above specification of the notion of abstraction entails that the (conceptual) result of an observational process is set apart, or separated, from the original process. In this respect, a significant contrast obtains between the conceptual structuring of, and the abstraction from, the world. In structuring the world, we focus on specific items of an overall observational process, and, in doing so, we necessarily leave out other possible items. However, the point of my approach is that in employing concepts in this way we structure a particular type of overall process, while in abstracting we focus exclusively on its result in order to transcend this particular type of process. It is only in the latter case that we can sensibly speak of abstraction, since it involves not just leaving out but also setting apart. By focusing on the result we set it apart from the process that produced it.

Thus both leaving out and setting apart should be taken into account in a philosophical analysis of the process of abstraction. To be sure, abstraction in the sense of leaving out and setting apart is not always a conscious activity. On the contrary, since this procedure is so common and so routinely practiced, it is more likely that, in the majority of cases, it will not be consciously noticed at all.

The third notion associated with abstraction is that of summarizing. Through this notion, abstraction is often closely connected to the issue of generality or universality. Thus, in the context of concept formation, abstraction is often seen as the procedure that gives us general or universal concepts. In this view, the process of concept formation starts with the direct or nonconceptual observation of a number of particular situations. By comparing these situations, that is to say, by leaving out the irrelevant particularities or idiosyncrasies and by mentally setting apart what is relevant and common, we abstract a general concept from its individual, spatiotemporal instantiations. This concept, then, abstractly represents all the particular situations of a certain kind. In addition, this conceptual representation is often taken to give us the essence of the kind. This view is usually called the classical doctrine of abstraction. It has been advocated, in varying interpretations, by Aristotle, Thomas Aquinas, John Locke, Wilhelm Wundt, Edmund Husserl, and Alfred Whitehead (see Blokhuis 1985, especially 40–42).

My account of observation necessitates rejecting this view of concept formation, however. The observation of particular situations is always conceptually interpreted right from the start. Hence conceiving of the process of abstraction as a kind of inferential procedure from directly given, uninterpreted particulars to their conceptual, general representations is inadequate. Clearly, this critique amounts to endorsing the view that concepts structure the world, which implies that the notion of abstraction in the sense of summarizing is inadequate.[2]

Of course, this Kantian view is by no means original, and it has been extensively discussed by many philosophers in various philosophical contexts (see, for instance, Hacking 1975, 57–66). Koningsveld also belongs to the Kantian tradition. As we have seen, his approach implies that concepts produce or increase order in initially less well-structured observational situations and, more generally, that the world—in as far as it is empirically accessible—is a conceptually structured world. He contrasts this view with the classical theory of abstraction, according to which concepts are formed by abstracting from the irrelevant features of the particular situations (Koningsveld 1976, 132). On the basis of his account of the thob-urve-raig experiment, he claims that the decisive defect of this theory is that we first have to know which are the (ir)relevant features of a situation before we are able to abstract a concept. Thus, in the case of the thob-urve-raig experiment, we must know that the similarity of the figures to linguistic characters is not relevant, while their geometrical form is. But we can only know this if we have already acquired these aspects of the concept in question. Hence, Koningsveld concludes, concept formation by means of abstraction presupposes the availability of the very concept to be formed.

I agree with the general trend of this line of argument, but I think it needs to be slightly qualified. One might reply that the question of (ir)relevancy can be taken to be part of the process of abstraction and that it can be decided in the course of this process. What this shows, however, is that the real point of the Kantian argument is not so much that we need to answer the question of what is (ir)relevant in advance of the observation, but that it cannot be answered on the basis of an allegedly conceptually uninterpreted process of observation. For example, the fact that in the thob-urve-raig experiment similarity to linguistic characters is irrelevant cannot be abstracted from presumably uninterpreted, particular observations. The classical theory of abstraction presupposes the availability of the concept to be formed (or, more precisely, of certain of its crucial aspects) primarily in a logical and less so in a temporal sense. For this reason, the criticism of this theory still stands.

Abstract and Concrete

Another relevant issue is the contrast between abstract and concrete. In particular, the question is whether or not an extensible concept is abstract in the sense of not being concrete (or, similarly, not being direct or immediate).

In many philosophical views, abstract and concrete are opposed in an evaluative hierarchy. Thus in empiricism the two notions are ranked in a semantic or epistemological hierarchy. The truth of abstract theoretical claims is seen to be questionable, and hence such claims require an explicit philosophical justification; concrete empirical claims, in contrast, are taken to be the unproblematic starting points of philosophical analysis. Phenomenology and hermeneutics, to mention two other schools of thought, often stress the personal or sociocultural priority of concrete experience over the so-called abstractions of theoretical science. From such philosophical perspectives, the process of abstraction and its result, the abstract, have a limited significance only. According to empiricists, abstractions are in need of justification in terms of the experience of concrete particulars. And, according to phenomenological and hermeneutical philosophers, abstraction should be constrained and controlled by the life world of concrete people and their "rich" experiences and traditions. The spirit of the latter view is well captured by the title and subtitle of Paul Feyerabend's (1999) posthumously published book *Conquest of Abundance: A Tale of Abstraction versus the Richness of Being.*

In contrast, the account proposed here does not imply such a hierarchical and value-laden opposition between the abstract and the concrete. First, the empiricist appeal to a level of experience that would be concrete in the sense of being direct or immediate, and hence could serve as a taken-for-granted foundation for semantics or epistemology, is untenable because all observation is necessarily conceptually interpreted. Furthermore, the idea of abstraction as a leaving out of the particular realization context of a concept with a view to possibly realizing it in a new context, bears no exclusive relation to "abstract" science. It applies as much to the most mundane, ordinary concepts (such as "red" or "thob") as it does to the most esoteric, scientific ones (such as "isospin" or "solar neutrino"). Of course, the fact that all extensible concepts are abstract does not exclude that, in various other respects, smaller or larger differences between concepts may exist. Finally, this procedure of abstraction is definitely part of our concrete experience, since all of us are familiar with it and practice it when we aspire to extend a certain concept to a new situation. Consequently, it is difficult to see why such a fundamental and frequently practiced procedure should have only a limited philosophical and sociocultural significance.

Nonlocal Meanings, Human-Independent Potentialities, and Local Realizations

In addition to the issues of the process of abstraction and the contrast between abstract and concrete, there is the ontological question of the nature and existence of abstract entities. Are such entities implied in, or do they result from, processes of abstraction as sketched above? If so, what can be said about their nature and their existence? In discussing this question I make use of my earlier proposal of an ontology for the experimental sciences. Thus we first need a brief explanation of this ontology before we can address the question of the nature and existence of extensible concepts as abstract entities.

In Radder (1996, chap. 4) I argue, first, that a reproducible experiment has a nonlocal meaning that transcends the meaning of the local reproductions of the experiment that have been carried out so far. Second, I claim that, if the descriptive terms occurring in the conceptual-theoretical interpretation of a reproducible experiment refer, then they are about a persisting potentiality of a human-independent reality. Third, I conclude that the realization of such a potentiality essentially depends on local theoretical and material work; that is to say, particular realizations are historically situated, human achievements.[3]

My account of extensible concepts owes a great deal to the ontology of human-independent potentialities and reproducible experiments, with their nonlocal meanings and their historically situated realizations. More specifically, the notion of the extensibility of concepts can be seen to be a direct analogy of the idea of the replicability of experimental results. Replicability is a specific type of reproducibility, denoting the reproducibility of an experimental result by means of (possibly radically) different experimental processes.[4] A simple illustration is the result that "a fluid of type *f* has boiling point *b*," which may be realized through experimental processes that use various kinds of thermometers.

A more elaborate example can be found in Giacomo Morpurgo's searches for isolated quarks. His experiments, conducted between 1965 and 1980, were extensions of the classical oil-drop design by means of which Robert Millikan measured the electrical charge of the electron. Andrew Pickering provides the following account of this case.

> There were an *indefinite* number of ways in which Morpurgo could extend Millikan's example. And, in case I am accused of making philosophical points of no historical substance, I can note that Morpurgo did indeed explore all sorts of extensions in the real time of his experiments. He first sought to suspend particles of graphite (his equivalent of Millikan's oil drops) in a liquid in order to observe their response to an applied electric field and hence to determine their charges. Later he suspended them in a magnetic field; later still he suspended iron cylinders in a differently contrived magnetic field. And within the magnetic-suspension experiments many particular variations in material procedure were tried. (1995a, 48, emphasis added)[5]

More generally, the practice of scientific experimentation shows many cases of the replication (either by the original experimenter or by other experimenters) of a result by means of quite different experimental processes.

If a term that occurs in the statement of an experimentally replicable result refers, its referent can be described as "(a part of) the common result of an indeterminate set of experimental processes."[6] As before, the set is indeterminate because it includes the potentially realizable processes. I call this referent a nonlocal.[7] Analogously, one may say that if an extensible concept refers, then it refers to a nonlocal. Again, this nonlocal can be described as "(a part of) the common result of an indeterminate set of observational processes." For instance, if the extensible concept "raig" that occurs in the replicable result "type X figures are raig" refers, then it refers to a nonlocal.

In sum, the categories of this ontology can be characterized as follows.

First, the potentialities of nature are human independent. If there were no human beings, the potentialities of nature would still be there. Perhaps aliens could realize them in ways that radically differ from ours. But it is improbable that there would be concepts if no humans (or no anthropoids) existed.[8] Furthermore, the meaning of extensible concepts transcends the meaning of all the local processes in which they have been realized so far. Thus nonlocal meanings cannot be identified with the meanings of a particular set of local realizations. The latter realizations, in which the concepts have actually been used thus far, are historically situated, human achievements. The conclusion is that human-independent potentialities, extensible concepts with their nonlocal meanings, and local realizations of particular observational processes constitute sui generis ontological categories that cannot be reduced to each other.

Extensible Concepts as Abstract Entities

Now that these ontological issues have been clarified, I can finally address the subject of the nature and existence of abstract entities and, in particular, the question of whether extensible concepts constitute such abstract entities. In many accounts, abstract entities are characterized in two ways.[9] First, abstract entities are said to exist outside of space and time, and thus to lack spatiotemporal properties and relations. Numbers and universals are often taken to exemplify such entities. Second, abstract entities are claimed to be "dependent entities" in the sense that it is logically impossible for them to exist separately from some other entity or entities. Thus, although this specific apple and its particular color can be separated mentally, this individual color is an abstract particular that cannot really exist independently from the apple. Clearly, according to these criteria, abstractness is not something that comes in degrees: entities are either abstract or not abstract. In contrast, in ordinary usage a particular thing may be said to be more (or less) abstract than something else.

Are extensible concepts and their referents, the nonlocals, abstract entities according to the two criteria set out above?[10] Consider first the nonlocal referent of a specific extensible concept, for instance, of the concept of "type X raigness," that is to say, the raigness of all possible type X figures. I describe this kind of entity as (a part of) the common result of an indeterminate set of potentially realizable observational processes. As we have seen, the idea of nonlocality is closely connected to the notions of indeterminacy and modality. In the future, type X raigness might be realized as part of the result of various novel observational processes. But so far these processes are mere potentialities. This modal aspect of nonlocals implies that they are outside of space and time, and hence abstract, in the specific sense that it is indeterminate whether or not (the results of) these observational processes can or will ever be realized in actual space and time. On the second criterion, nonlocals prove to be abstract as well. Even if a nonlocal, by definition, transcends the processes in which it has been realized so far, it is not sensible to grant it existence independently of any realization process.[11]

The latter claim can be rephrased as saying that nonlocals emerge from their local realizations. Recently, quite a few philosophers have discussed the notion of emergence (see, for example, Kim 1999). Many of those discussions, however, attempt to squeeze this notion into a "nonreductive" physicalist framework. This framework allows for the emergence of particular novel entities or properties, but ontologically such emergent entities or properties are still physical. Thus a particular fluid, or a particular fluidity, may emerge from a certain constellation of specific molecules, but ontologically speaking this fluid is a perfectly normal physical entity and this fluidity a perfectly normal physical property. As I argue elsewhere, however, the doctrine of ontological, nonreductive physicalism is fraught with fundamental and insoluble problems (see Radder 2001). Hence, in contrast to physicalist accounts of emergence, my claim is that emergence may create genuine ontological novelty. Thus, in the case of extensible concepts, their referents—the emergent nonlocals—are abstract, and therefore nonphysical, but nonetheless real.[12]

Interestingly enough, this account of the referents of specific extensible concepts can also be applied to the concept of extensible concepts itself. The reason is that the realization and potential extension of the concept of "extensible concept" can be construed in complete analogy to the realization

Sign	Different tokens of the type of sign	Concept	Referent
X	x X **X**	"type X raigness"	(a part of) the common result of an indeterminate set of potentially realizable observational processes of raig figures of type X
extensible concept	extensible concept EXTENSIBLE CONCEPT uitbreidbaar begrip	"extensible concept"	(a part of) the common result of an indeterminate set of potentially realizable observational processes of a type of material/linguistic signs

TABLE 10.1. The analogy between "type X raigness" and "extensible concept."

and potential extension of specific concepts (such as "type X raigness"). Put differently, the concept of "extensible concept" is itself extensible.

To see this, think of a concept as itself abstracted from behavioral linguistic processes. From this perspective, we may conceive of reading or hearing as an observational process, and of reading or hearing a particular (written or spoken) word or phrase as (a part of) the result of the process.[13] This particular word or phrase may be called the material/linguistic sign of an extensible concept, in the same way as X may be called a sign of the concept of raigness. That is to say, the extensible concept itself coincides neither with the particular material signs nor with the particular linguistic signs that have been used to express it so far. If I changed all the characters of this word-processed document into capitals, the material sign of the concept of "extensible concept" would be different. And if I decided to call it "*uitbreidbaar begrip*" (its Dutch equivalent), the linguistic sign (the word) would be modified. Yet, the meaning of the concept of "extensible concept" would not be affected by these changes.[14]

On this basis, the referent of the concept of "extensible concept" can be defined as "(a part of) the common result of an indeterminate set of potentially realizable observational processes of a type of material/linguistic signs." If we replace, in this definition, "a type of material/linguistic signs" by "raig figures of type X," the analogy between the concept "extensible concept" and the concept "type X raigness" is evident. Table 10.1 summarizes the different aspects of this analogy.

In conclusion, since the set of novel realizations of the signs of a concept is indeterminate, the extensible concept refers to a nonlocal or—as I have phrased it—the extensible concept possesses a nonlocal meaning. Because of this indeterminacy, concepts do not exist within space and time. Furthermore, the fact that there are no isolated nonlocals implies that the meaning of a concept cannot exist independently of any material or linguistic sign. Thus, because their meaning does not coincide with the meaning of the set of their local realizations and because they cannot exist independently of any realization whatsoever, extensible concepts are abstract entities.

WIDER PHILOSOPHICAL IMPLICATIONS

The notions of extensible concepts, abstraction, and nonlocals have several fundamental and far-reaching philosophical implications. Here I discuss some of these implications, including their relation and relevance to other philosophical issues and views, to further clarify and vindicate the claim that concepts both structure the world and abstract from it.

Concepts and Communication

A central conclusion from the discussion of extensible concepts is that they are abstract and that their meaning is nonlocal because it does not coincide with the meaning of a fixed set of local processes in which the concepts have been used so far. Put differently, the meaning of extensible concepts cannot be reduced to their past and present uses. The basic intuition that lies at the root of this approach is that (the linguistic expressions of) concepts cannot and should not be literal representations of determinate local processes. After all, local observational processes may, and often do, differ significantly from each other in various respects, as in the case of the thob-urve-raig experiment and its proposed replication. Hence concepts and languages would be useless for extension to novel situations and for communication with people in novel situations if their meaning were strongly dependent on the particularities of specific observational processes.

Quite a few contemporary views concerning the issues in question, however, show a strong or even an exclusive emphasis on the philosophical significance of local practices. This obviously applies to constructivist and postmodern approaches (for instance, Latour 1987; Rouse 1987; Pickering 1995b), but it also holds for certain naturalist views (for example, Churchland 1989). I take their point into account through the notion of the local realization of observational processes. If we confine ourselves to the locality perspective, however, we lack an adequate philosophical account of the actual and possible connections between these separate local practices (compare with Nickles 1989, 328–30). The idea of the extensibility of concepts and their nonlocal meanings is meant to provide such an account for the case of the formation and use of concepts. Central to this account is the claim that, in a specific sense, concepts abstract from the world.

It is illuminating to briefly compare this account with Bertrand Russell's views of the nature and function of language and meaning. On the one hand, Russell agrees that local situations may and often do vary in significant respects. He also claims that one important function of language is to connect these different local situations. "Without language, only that part of our life which consists of public sensations would be communicable, and that only to those so situated as to be able to share the sensations in question" (1948, 59 60).

On the other hand, starting from a strongly empiricist viewpoint, he holds that language is primarily acquired "by acquaintance" with a local situation and, more importantly, that the meaning of linguistic expressions is given by their referents in this local situation. Together with the claim that local situations often differ substantially, this leads him to conclude that meaning is essentially private. "It would be absolutely fatal if people meant the same things by their words. It would make all intercourse impossible, and language the most hopeless and useless thing imaginable, because the meaning you attach to your words must depend on the nature of the objects you are acquainted with, and since different people are acquainted with different objects, they would not be able to talk to each other unless they attached quite different meanings to their words" (Russell 1956, 195).

Unfortunately, the conclusion that meaning is essentially based on private acquaintance entails the irresolvable problem of how communication between people in different situations can ever succeed at all. Hence the view that concepts and their linguistic expressions both structure the world and abstract from it must avoid this problem. It does so, first, by siding with Gottlob Frege, Hilary Putnam, and Ian Hacking, among others, in claiming that a theory of meaning should include an explanation of the possibility of public discourse (see Hacking 1975; Putnam 1975; Visser 1991; Stokhof

2000, chap. 1). Meaning has an irreducibly public and social dimension, and language cannot be adequately interpreted in terms of local reference only. Second, I agree with Russell (1956, 196) that communication is possible only because concepts and language are "ambiguous." This ambiguity, however, does not result from the fact that meanings are entirely private or local but rather from the fact that they are indeterminate and open ended. The latter implies that the meaning of concepts needs to be articulated when they are being extended or communicated to a novel situation. Russell (196) argues that "if you were to insist on language which was unambiguous, you would be unable to tell people at home what you had seen in foreign parts." On my account, because of the ambiguity—that is to say, the nonlocality—of the meaning of concepts, we are never able to offer home a literal description of what we have seen in foreign parts.[1] What is being communicated is not the local experience of an entire observational process by the sender but a "result" that has to be incorporated into the observational experience of the receiver, which can be expected to be more or less different from that of the sender.

Drawing on the work of Jacques Derrida, Simon Glendinning advocates an interesting view of language and communication that is—to a certain extent and at a general level—comparable to my approach. While taking account of the connection between language and its contextual uses, he emphasizes the essential "iterability" of linguistic expressions. "The point is not that linguistic elements (of which it makes sense to say that they can be applied only once) can (also), as a matter of brute fact or as a fortuitous eventuality, find application on more than one occasion, but that the applicability-on-occasions-other-than-this-one *constitutes* their being what they are" (Glendinning 2000, 277; see also Berns 1979; Roothaan 2005, chap. 3). On this basis, Glendinning argues against the assumption that the content of communications is, or can be, fully unambiguous and determinate.

In spite of these similarities, certain differences obtain as well. First, the Derridean account does not include a detailed explanation of the mechanism through which this iterability comes about in practice. More important, however, is that the structuring role of concepts and language is completely absent from this account of communication and writing.

Nonlocals and Universals

Nonlocals are the referents of extensible concepts, and my account of observational processes implies that *all* extensible concepts refer to nonlocals. In the case of concepts expressed by property terms, the notion of a nonlocal is analogous to that of a universal in more traditional ontologies (compare with Moreland 2001). The change from universal to nonlocal derives from the proposed account of observational processes. More precisely, it is a consequence of the fact that properties may be realized in various ways through contingent observational processes.

Apart from this, there is a further difference between universals and nonlocals. In contrast to universals, nonlocals can be of various types. For instance, both the property term "thob" and the object term "electron" refer to a nonlocal. The meaning not only of property terms but also of object terms transcends the meaning they have as interpretations of the observational processes in which they have been realized so far.

This discussion also demonstrates that talk of nonlocals is more than "covert talk of language," as might be suggested in analogy to Rudolf Carnap's linguistic interpretation of universals (1952). Indeed, my talk of nonlocals essentially includes an analysis of how observational processes are realized by (groups of) people. If we want to obtain an adequate account of the formation and use of concepts and their relation to the world, we have to talk both in the substantive, material mode and in the metalinguistic, formal mode. In other words, we must go beyond a purely metalinguistic approach to these ontological questions by including an account of the actual and potential realization of observational processes.

Abstract Concepts and Popperian World-Three Entities

To further clarify the account of extensible concepts, abstraction, and nonlocals, I contrast it with Karl Popper's views of abstract entities. In his "epistemology without a knowing subject," which he defines as a theory of scientific knowledge, Popper considers the epistemological and, especially, the ontological status of problem situations, arguments, and theories (1972).

He situates these entities in what he calls world-three, and sharply distinguishes them from the physical and mental objects or states that populate world-one and world-two. The relations among world-three entities are of a logical nature, while world-one entities are connected through physical relations and world-two entities through mental relations.

World-three entities, even if they are human products and although they interact with entities from world-one and world-two, may exist independently from these latter worlds. Thus a crucial feature of world-three is its autonomy, which results from a process of self-transcendence. "I suggest that everything depends upon the give-and-take between ourselves and our work; upon the product which we contribute to the third world, and upon that constant feed-back that can be amplified by conscious self-criticism. The incredible thing about life, evolution and mental growth, is just this method of give-and-take, this interaction between our actions and their results by which we constantly transcend ourselves, our talents, our gifts" (Popper 1972, 147).

My account of the meaning of concepts also entails a notion of transcendence. Extensible concepts, which have been applied to a restricted class of observational processes, possess a nonlocal meaning that transcends the meaning they have as interpretations of the results of these particular processes. Thus at this general level a similarity obtains between Popper's world-three entities and extensible concepts as abstract entities.

In spite of this, there are also several important dissimilarities. First, in claiming that world-three products are "much more important and fundamental" than world-two processes, Popper tries to establish a hierarchical relationship between these worlds. His main argument for the existence of such a hierarchy is that the impact of world-three "on any one of us, even on the most original of creative thinkers, vastly exceeds the impact which any of us can make upon it" (1972, 147). This argument, however, presupposes that world-two knowledge is the knowledge of individual human beings. If we take into account the collective dimension of the production of world-two knowledge—for instance, through scientific communities—the argument for the primacy of world-three breaks down. Indeed, from a Kuhnian perspective, Popper's thesis (1972, 112) that a study of the process of knowledge production by scientists cannot teach us anything about the status of problems, arguments, or theories is downright implausible.

Another striking feature of Popper's epistemology without a knowing subject is its virtual silence about the role of the physical (or, as I prefer to say, the material) world-one in the production of knowledge. The theory focuses exclusively on world-two and world-three and on their relationship. Apparently, Popper assumes it to be feasible to construct a theory of knowledge of the (material) world without taking explicit account of our interaction with that world. Consequently, his notion of self-transcendence is quite similar to the Hegelian notion of an individual consciousness that transcends itself into a world of objective ideas. In contrast, what is being transcended through nonlocal meanings is a set of local material realizations and their conceptual interpretations. These realizations and interpretations include, in Popper's terms, both world-one and world-two processes.

A further point is also related to the issue of transcendence. An important—and basically correct—argument of Popper against the interpretation of knowledge in terms of subjective belief is that human knowledge always has unforeseen logical consequences. A scientific theory, for example, will have implications of which nobody is aware at a particular time, or of which nobody may ever be aware. Logically speaking, however, at any particular time the content of world-three is fixed. This logical closure of world-three, at a specific moment, entails another contrast with the notion of transcendence implied by the theory of nonlocal meaning. The reason for the nonlocality of the meaning of concepts is not that individuals are not (yet) aware of all the logical consequences of those concepts. Rather, extensible concepts are genuinely open ended because their meaning depends on fundamentally contingent, possible realizations and conceptualizations.

Finally, Popper (1972, 123–24) claims that arguments, theories, truth, and the like constitute the philosophically interesting notions, while words, concepts, and meanings are unimportant. His argument for this claim is not that clear, though. He tells us that all philosophers who think that words, concepts, and their meaning are significant notions suffer from "the problem of universals." He seems to construe this problem as the attempt to derive and justify concepts and their meaning on the basis of pure, uninterpreted experience. Such a derivation and justification is then claimed to be impossible because universal concepts structure experience and cannot be reduced to it (see also Popper 1959, 93–95). In contrast, I demonstrate in the previous chapters, first, that the problem of the relationship between concepts and the world is significant and cannot be dismissed as easily as it is done by Popper and, second, that it is possible to formulate a plausible view of the meaning of concepts that is not based on the classical theory of abstraction and that is compatible with the Popperian claim that concepts structure the world.

The Dynamics of Concept Development

Consider again the contrast between structuring the world and abstracting from it. As we have seen, the view that concepts structure the world is not, strictly speaking, wrong. Yet it may easily lead to inadequate accounts of the role of concepts in cognitive processes. This is obviously the case in those Kantian views in which all structuring concepts are taken to be unchangeable and universally valid. These views entail an essentially static picture, for instance, of the perception of space through universal Euclidean concepts or of the observation of color through a unique classification scheme. Consequently, they have great difficulties in accommodating the variability and historicity of concepts that are documented in an ever-increasing number of anthropological and historical studies.[2]

A more dynamic view results if one stresses the essential fallibility of our attempts to structure the world. Thus more Popperian approaches emphasize the fact that our conceptual structurings may meet with refutations, anomalies, exceptions, and the like. In this spirit, Herman Koningsveld writes, "Fortunately genuine exceptions do occur and they make our concepts fertile by initiating further investigation, thereby determining *empirical inquiry as a dynamic undertaking*" (1973, 24; see also Koningsveld 1976, 139–54).

According to Koningsveld, the best strategy for coping with exceptions— that is, or should be, followed in science—is to see them as heuristic opportunities for specifying and developing our concepts by looking for a systematic explanation of the anomalies in question. Be that as it may, the account of extending concepts by way of abstraction implies that the dynamics of conceptual development is not restricted to the strategy of taking exceptions seriously. In particular, this account shows that there is a dynamics of concept formation and articulation that does not have to await the occurrence of exceptions or anomalies. Concepts possess an intrinsic open-endedness that enables their extension to novel situations without being dependent on a prior clash with actual counterexamples.

Abstraction, Operationalization, and Idealization

Extensible concepts have a nonlocal meaning, which transcends the meaning they possess in virtue of the way they have been used so far in interpreting the result of a particular set of observational processes. At first sight, this claim appears to be similar to the criticisms that have been leveled at the operationalist theory of meaning in the philosophy of science. Impressed by the achievements of Einstein's theory of special relativity, the main originator of operationalism, P. W. Bridgman, held that concepts can and should be completely defined by the set of operations that are used to measure their values. "We may illustrate by considering the concept of length: what do we mean by the length of an object? We evidently know what we mean by length if we can tell what the length of any and every object is, and for the physicist nothing more is required. To find the length of an object we have to perform certain operations. The concept of length is therefore fixed when the operations by which length is measured are fixed" (1961, 5). One consequence of this view is that the concept of length as determined by means of a measuring rod is not the same as that measured by means of a light ray: "We must recognize in principle that in changing the operations we have really changed the concept" (Bridgman 1961, 23).

The operationalist theory of meaning has had a considerable impact on science, though less on physics than on behaviorist psychology and social science. In philosophy of science, however, operationalism has been severely criticized (see, e.g., Hempel 1966, 88–100; Kroes 1996, 143–46). According to its critics, the basic defect of operationalism is that it leads to a pointless proliferation of concepts. Consequently, it cannot do justice to the systematic significance of concepts and conceptual or theoretical frameworks. Concepts in theoretical science, it is claimed, have a sui generis meaning that cannot be reduced to the procedures by which they are measured.

From my perspective, this critique of the operationalist theory of meaning requires a qualified response.[3] I fully agree with the claim that the meaning of a theoretical concept cannot be reduced to a specific measuring procedure. However, the problem with this claim is not only that it leads to a pointless proliferation of concepts, but also that it implies that the meaning of concepts is essentially static. Thus operationalism also fails to acknowledge the intrinsic open-endedness of concepts. It is this open-endedness that enables the extensibility and communicability of concepts to completely novel situations. Hence the account of extensible concepts and their nonlocal meanings specifies an important procedure through which concepts *acquire* a systematic import.

However, even if the meaning of a concept cannot be fully reduced to specific measurement operations, this meaning does depend on such procedures. After all, the meaning of concepts that are supposed to tell us something about the world cannot be determined on the basis of theoretical definitions only. Hence, as I conclude at the beginning of chapter 10, the structuring meaning component of a concept will change when the concept is successfully extended to a substantially novel domain. A successful replication of Koningsveld's experiment in the new domain of the blind students will (slightly) shift the meaning of the concepts of thob, urve, and raig. However, because such extension processes lead to a shift, or change, in the meaning of a concept, rather than to a completely new concept, an important contrast with operationalism remains.

Finally, the earlier criticisms of operationalism, for instance, by Carl Hempel, were based on a distinction between empirical and theoretical concepts, and they implied the inadequacy of operationalism for theoretical concepts only. In contrast, the account of the nonlocality of meaning does not presuppose such a distinction: it applies to any extensible concept that may occur in the interpretation of observational processes, be it an "empirical" concept such as "red" or a "theoretical" concept such as "solar neutrino."

I close this chapter with a few remarks on the relation between abstraction and idealization, in particular with respect to science. These two notions are often treated as being closely connected or even as being almost identical.[4] No doubt this usage is a consequence of the fact that many discussions of abstraction focus on mathematics and its function in science. Thus the geometrical circle is said to be an abstract idealization of the concrete circles that populate the material world. A related example can be found in debates on the role of mathematics in scientific theories. Here one regularly comes across the view that abstract theories represent the phenomena in the same idealized way as maps represent geographical areas (see, for example, Toulmin 1967, chap. 4).

My discussion of the notion of abstraction analyzes it primarily in terms of leaving out and setting apart. In particular, I argue that in attempting to extend a concept we leave out from the conceptual interpretation of the original observational process everything but its result, and, in doing so, we set apart this result as potentially realizable through one or more different observational processes. This formulation shows quite clearly that no intrinsic relation between abstraction and idealization is implied here. Indeed, abstraction in this sense applies to any extensible concept whatsoever. Idealization is different. Think for a moment about the paradigmatic case of the relation between a concrete, material circle and its mathematical idealization. In this case, it will be clear that idealization does not work through a combined leaving out and setting apart, but is primarily a matter of approximation. The concrete, material circle is replaced by a mathematical one, preferably in such a way that the geometrical differences between the two are small or negligible. Consequently, a process of idealization will be acceptable so long as the relevant properties of the idealized entities approximate the corresponding properties of the concrete, material entities to a sufficient degree. In contrast, in processes of abstraction, as conceptualized in this book, the notion of approximation plays no role at all. Moreover, when we are aware of the idealizations we make, we know that they cannot be literally true. Claims involving abstract, extensible concepts, however, may be either true or false. This fact marks another important distinction between idealizations and abstractions.

ABSTRACTION, FORMALIZATION, AND DIGITIZATION

In chapter 10, I briefly mention the idea of a proposition as an abstract entity presupposed in formal logic and formal semantics. Often, being formal and being abstract are seen as closely related to each other, and the same applies to the processes of formalization and abstraction (see, e.g., Franklin 1994). This raises the question of the relationship between formalization and the specific notion of abstraction introduced in the previous chapters. I examine this relationship by means of a discussion and assessment of John Haugeland's account of formal systems and the formal concepts they include. He closely connects formal and digital systems and uses both notions to argue for the feasibility of artificial intelligence. Thus the focus of this chapter is on the use of formal systems and concepts in artificial intelligence research and not, for instance, in mathematics. I conclude that Haugeland's notion of formal systems, including that of formal concepts, is highly problematic, and I show that this critique does not apply to abstract, extensible concepts, in spite of the prima facie similarities between formalization and abstraction.

The aim of Haugeland's book (1987) is to explain and vindicate the classical approach to artificial intelligence as the rule-guided manipulation of the formal symbols of the "language of thought." He dubs this approach GOFAI (good old-fashioned artificial intelligence). Thus this account of formal systems is not merely Haugeland's personal view but representative of a large group of writers in the area of artificial intelligence. (The more recent connectionist approach to the study of artificial intelligence, or, more broadly, of cognitive processes constitutes the most prominent alternative to the symbol manipulation approach. See Bechtel and Abrahamsen 1991, chap. 1; Olazaran 1996.)

In the symbol manipulation approach, the notion of a formal system plays a central role. Haugeland introduces and characterizes formal systems by comparing them to a certain type of game. "A *formal system* is like a game in which tokens are manipulated according to rules, in order to see what configurations can be obtained. In fact, many familiar games—among them chess, checkers, Chinese checkers, go, and tic-tac-toe—simply *are* formal systems. But other games—such as marbles, tiddlywinks, billiards and baseball—aren't formal at all. . . . What's the difference? All formal games have three essential features (not shared by other games): they are 'token manipulation' games; they are 'digital'; and they are 'finitely playable'" (Haugeland 1987, 48). Thus formal systems are similar to, though not identical to, formal games. The main difference between the two is that the former are not always competitive and do not always have goals or winning positions (Haugeland 1987, 50–51).

Formal systems evolve through the rule-guided manipulation of tokens. The tokens are the individual pieces or, more generally, the individual objects with which the game is played. By manipulating the tokens we transform one position of the game into another. Tokens can be of one type, such as the pieces in checkers, or of various types, such as the rooks and the pawns in chess. Ultimately, the rules of the game determine the meaning of its types of token. More particularly, the rules specify, first, the starting position(s), that is, the initial configuration(s) of the tokens; second, the legal moves, that is, the allowed manipulations of the (different types of) tokens from one position to another; and third, the goal position(s) of the game, that is, the configuration or configurations that entail that the game has been completed.

The second key feature of a formal system is its digitalness. In digital systems, there are prespecified types that enable the unambiguous identification and—if the system has more than one type—classification of the tokens. This lack of ambiguity results from two facts. First, the tokens of a digitized game may be realized in a variety of ways without ceasing to be identical, that is, without ceasing to be tokens of the same type. Thus individual chess pawns may be brand new or well worn, of smaller or larger sizes, or stylized in this or that specific way, but they still remain tokens of the same type. A ten-euro bank note, to give another example, may be dirty and damaged and still have the same cash value as a newly printed ten-euro note. The second fact that accounts for the lack of ambiguity of a digital system is that its types are discrete. This implies that tokens of two different types are, and should be, clearly distinct. Thus in chess there is a clear distinction between a pawn and a rook, and within the money system, a ten-euro note is obviously distinct from a twenty-euro note.

More particularly, Haugeland goes on, playing a digital token manipulation game is based on two specific techniques. "A *digital system* is a set of positive and reliable techniques (methods, devices) for producing and reidentifying tokens, or configurations of tokens, from some prespecified set of types" (Haugeland 1987, 53). A positive technique is one that, in principle, can succeed totally or perfectly; a reliable technique is one that, in practice, is likely to succeed. Thus counting a number of prespecified objects (for instance, the ballpoints on my desk) is a technique which is both positive and reliable. Dividing each of those objects in two parts of exactly equal weight is not positive, while it may or may not be reliable, depending on the availability of adequate cutting and weighing tools and on our tolerance for inaccuracies. Thus formal games, being digital by definition, should be based on positive and reliable techniques. According to Haugeland, games such as chess constitute straightforward examples of formal games.

The third feature of a formal system is its finite playability. This feature guarantees that formal games are playable by finite players and thus feasible in practice. This means, more concretely, that the procedure for proposing a move (or showing that there is none), as well as the procedure for determining whether or not the proposed move would be legal, can be completed within a finite time.

On the basis of the definition of formal systems by these three features, Haugeland (1987, 58–63) draws two important conclusions. First, he claims that formal systems are medium independent. That is to say, the identity of a digitized token does not depend on the specific ways it has been materially realized. Chess may be played on an ordinary board with ordinary wooden pieces. But it might also be played with thirty-two radio-controlled helicopter "pieces" (of the required types) and a "board" consisting of sixty-four suitably located rooftops. Second, this medium independence allows the application of the notion of formal equivalence to token manipulation games. Two games of chess that are materially realized in different ways are nevertheless formally equivalent if they constitute the same formal system. Ordinary and helicopter chess, for example, are formally equivalent to each other.

Finally, Haugeland uses the results of his analysis of formal systems to explain his approach to the problem of artificial intelligence. He defines computers as "interpreted automatic formal systems" and posits the fundamental equivalence of human and artificial (or computer) intelligence. "The notions of medium independence and formal equivalence are crucially important to Artificial Intelligence and to computational psychology in general. . . . Brain cells and electronic circuits are manifestly different 'media'; but, maybe, at some appropriate level of abstraction, they can be media for equivalent formal systems. In that case, a computer mind might be as much a real (genuine) mind as helicopter (or computer) chess is genuine chess, only in a different medium" (Haugeland 1987, 63).[1]

Assessing the Relationship between Formal Systems and the World

In my discussion and assessment of Haugeland's views I focus on the first two characteristics of formal systems: the features of token manipulation and digitalness. The idea of finite playability and the definition of a computer as an interpreted automatic formal system are less directly relevant to the problem of the relationship between formalization and abstraction. The basic issue of this section is how and to what extent formal systems are related to the material world. What I mean here is not primarily the relationship between software and hardware but rather the problem of the applicability of formal systems to specific material systems and processes. For example, how are such formal systems connected to particular, materially realized token manipulation games? Answering such questions is important because it tells us what formal systems—and hence artificial intelligences—can, or cannot, achieve when they are applied to concrete practical problems.

First, consider Haugeland's claim that formal systems are (like) token manipulation games. The tokens are the individual material pieces or objects with which the game is played, such as the wooden or helicopter chess pieces. A basic feature of formal systems is, however, that the manifest characteristics and meanings the tokens have because of their being particular things located at particular places and times are irrelevant. Since the formal system itself is medium independent, the only characteristics and meanings that matter are the type, or formal, characteristics and meanings of the tokens, which are fixed by the rules. Hence a formal system cannot be identified with any of its concrete material realizations or even with the sum of all existing realizations. For this reason, to characterize formal systems as token manipulation games is inadequate. Essential to formal systems is the manipulation of "formal tokens," or symbols. Hence formal systems are better characterized as symbol manipulation games.

More is at stake in this ambiguity than mere terminology. When formal systems are said to be token manipulation games, the suggestion is that, although they are formal, they are nevertheless securely fastened to the material world of the concrete tokens. If they involve primarily symbol manipulation, though, their relationship to the material world is far less clear. For example, in practice the manipulation of concrete, material tokens may present all sorts of problems. This even applies to the games Haugeland mentions. Thus I remember quite well the difficulties I used to have in trying to play a particular game of Chinese checkers: either the pegs tended to stick to my fingers or they constantly toppled over (the latter was especially annoying when I tried to play the game during long and boring train trips). In practical chess playing, to mention another example, disputes about whether a move has been started—by touching the piece in question—or completed—by letting it go—are not exceptional (compare with Collins 1990, 25–26). In addition, the frequent and intentional employment of psychological strategies in playing chess refutes Haugeland's claim that this game is a purely formal system. This means that, to make chess and comparable games formally playable, the nonformalizable elements first need to be eliminated by transforming the way those games are being practiced.[2]

To be sure, Haugeland has not completely overlooked such problems. Thus he mentions that the tokens need to be both robust enough and not impossibly heavy or fixed to make real-time token manipulation possible

(Haugeland 1987, 60). However, in his overall approach to artificial intelligence he appears to take these problems for granted. First, he continues to speak of (full) medium independence as the major characteristic of formal systems. Furthermore, he does not take into account the nonpositive aspects of allegedly formal games, such as the role of psychological strategies in playing chess. Finally, in his explanation of the notion of digitalness he emphasizes the significance of positive techniques, which guarantee the playability of formal games in principle, but a systematic treatment of the issue of the reliability of playing these games, which determines their practical feasibility, is conspicuously absent. In sum, the bottom line of formalist artificial intelligence is that "formal systems are *self-contained;* the 'outside world' (anything not included in the current position) is strictly irrelevant" (Haugeland 1987, 50).

The second way formal types and material tokens are claimed to be connected is by means of the notion of digitalness. It is the digitalness of the tokens that is said to "underlie and make feasible" the medium independence of formal systems (Haugeland 1987, 57–60). Thus in this account digitalness forms the crucial link between the tokens of a particular game and the medium-independent formal system.

In fact, however, the relation between digitalness and medium independence is less tight and more contingent than Haugeland suggests. That is to say, games may be digital but not medium independent, and they may be medium independent but not digital. The former case is illustrated by games of chess in which, by stipulation, only wooden pieces and a wooden board of strictly specified shapes and colors are allowed. An example of the latter case would be the (fictional) cut-into-two-pieces-of-equal-weight game, the goal of which might be to find out who possesses the most accurate cutting skills. This game is medium independent, since it may be played with any object and any cutting technique, but it is not digital.

The underlying problem is that digitalness is a property ascribed to the physical tokens of a particular game, whereas the medium independence of rule-guided symbol manipulation is based on the stipulated or conventional autonomy of the system of rules. This entails, among other things, that Haugeland's claim that since the alphabet is digital, poems are medium independent cannot be correct. Consider, for instance, two material realizations of a poem, one (in ordinary characters) "chiseled in stone" and the other "embossed in Braille" (see Haugeland 1987, 59). In this case, there are two completely different alphabets. Hence it is obvious that it cannot be the (alleged) digitalness of either the ordinary or the Braille alphabet that underlies and makes feasible the formal equivalence of the two texts.[3] The reason Haugeland has not seen this is, I think, that he has confused the existence of a margin of tolerance in the case of digitized material tokens with the medium independence of formal types.

Harry Collins has provided an incisive criticism of the classical approach to artificial intelligence. In particular, he questions Haugeland's formalist approach for not taking into account the social processes through which tokens are made digital. "It is not symbols, or tokens by themselves that preserve and carry meaning. When we consider the way we interact with symbols and tokens they appear far more ambiguous and far less fixed. Their fixedness is at best a matter of the way we deal with them. To make the most crude of points, the value of a hand of cards depends on the opinion of the man with the gun, and the value of a base metal coin on the opinions of the people who make up the money markets" (1990, 25). I think that this specific critique is pertinent and should be taken seriously, even by those who do not agree with Collins's social-constructivist conclusions.

In spite of this, Collins seems to follow Haugeland in confusing the existence of a margin of tolerance of digitized tokens with the medium independence of formal types. Thus at one point he explicitly identifies formalization with digitization (1990, 49), and quite generally he treats formal systems as being basically systems of digitized tokens. More important, however, is that Collins's critique of formalization applies to the feature of digitization only, and hence the scope of this critique is limited to the structuring dimension of the use of formal concepts.

To summarize, formal systems are not simply token manipulation games, and the digitalness of particular tokens does not guarantee the medium independence of the formal types. Consequently, in the formalist approach the relationship between formal types and concrete material tokens is, in fact, taken for granted, and the adequacy of a formal system to its material realizations is actually postulated. This is also implicit in what Haugeland (1987, 106) calls the formalists' motto: "If you take care of the syntax, the semantics will take care of itself," where taking care of the syntax means playing the game according to its formal rules. However, if the adequacy of formal systems can be questioned even in the case of tightly structured games such as chess and Chinese checkers, it should certainly not be taken for granted in cases of far less structured human practices, such as the laboratory practice of crystal growing or the translation between natural languages (compare with Collins 1990).

Formalization and Abstraction

This discussion and evaluation of the notion of formal systems allows us to compare them with the abstractness of extensible concepts. Extensible concepts are abstract because they possess a nonlocal meaning. That is to say, this nonlocal meaning transcends the meaning the concepts have as interpretations of the results of the observational processes that have been realized so far. This formulation shows that there is a significant similarity between the nonlocal meaning of an extensible concept, such as "thob," and the medium-independent meaning of a formal concept, such as "pawn": the meaning of both sorts of concept is not fixed by the meaning of the processes/games in which they have been realized so far. It is precisely this similarity that motivates my comparison of abstraction and formalization. What remains to be shown, then, is that my criticisms of formal concepts do not apply to extensible concepts. This can be demonstrated by highlighting several important differences between the two sorts of concepts.

I argue in chapter 9 that applying extensible concepts requires the realization of entire observational processes and that, both practically and theoretically, the realizability of observational processes cannot be taken for granted. Thus practical issues in realizing such processes are fully accounted for, while theoretically extensibility is interpreted as a modal notion, denoting a possibility that may or may not prove to be realizable in actual practice. In contrast, formal artificial intelligence approaches take the practical problems of token manipulation largely for granted. In fact, these approaches conceptualize the playing of a game as a mere sequence of separate positions and not as a process of actual moves that need to be realized in practice.

Furthermore, I conclude that, if the connections between formal systems and concrete token manipulation games are taken seriously, formal concepts cannot be medium independent. In fact, the most that can be claimed for both formal and extensible concepts is that their meaning is nonlocal. Since nonlocality does not imply full medium independence, the problematic aspects of the latter notion are avoided.

Thus the medium independence of formal concepts reduces to the nonlocality of their meaning. If it were the case that digitalness is required for medium independence, the theory of nonlocal meaning would apply to digital signs only. But obviously not all signs of extensible concepts are necessarily digital. For instance, the signs of the thob-urve-raig concepts are clearly not digital. Fortunately, this is a pseudoproblem, since we have seen that the relationship between digitalness and medium independence is purely contingent. Hence there is no need at all to restrict the validity of the theory of nonlocal meaning to the (small) subset of those extensible concepts whose signs are digital.

13

In contemporary philosophical discourse, the notion of abstraction plays a less prominent role than it did in the past. No doubt this has to do with the increased currency of approaches that emphasize the structuring activities of human beings, either in a Kantian or in a more contextualized form. Nevertheless, exceptions to this trend occur. One such exception is Nancy Cartwright. Significantly enough, she places herself explicitly within the empiricist tradition. Thus the first sentence of her 1989 book, *Nature's capacities and their measurement*, reads, "Science is measurement."[1] As I note in chapter 10, from an empiricist point of view the (ontological, epistemological, or methodological) status of abstract entities, such as concepts and theories, naturally arises as an important issue.

Cartwright's focus is on science and, in particular, on the issue of causality and causal explanation in science (see Cartwright 1983). The subject of abstraction comes up in the context of her empiricist—but non-Humean—interpretation of causality (1989). She argues that modern scientific theories are about capacities and that abstraction is a critical factor in the construction of such theories. Furthermore, she offers detailed arguments for the existence and measurability of causal capacities. In her more recent work (1999), she adds that theories provide knowledge of the natures of things and that it is by virtue of those natures that things have the capacities they have. Generally speaking, knowledge of natures only tells us what things tend to do and hence what can happen. It is only in quite specific situations—such as the artificially controlled laboratory conditions—that this knowledge tells us what will actually happen.[2]

Cartwright's general account of science is worthwhile and stimulating. I briefly discuss her views to further clarify the notion of abstraction introduced in the previous chapters. Hence my focus is on the issue of abstraction, and I deal with her views of causality, capacities, and natures only in so far as it is directly relevant to my purposes.

In Cartwright's account, the notions of abstract and concrete are applied not only to concepts but also to claims, statements, and theories. She provides the following illustrations. As to the abstractness of concepts, the concept of the electrostatic coulomb force is said to be abstract as compared to the description of the spatiotemporal motion of two electrically charged particles at a distance r. An illustration from ordinary life is the more abstract concept of work as compared to the more concrete notions of dish washing or writing a grant proposal (Cartwright 1999, 39–40). Two examples of abstract claims or statements are "aspirins relieve headaches" and "an inversion in a population of atoms causes a narrow-band and coherent amplification in an applied signal" (the latter is the fundamental operating principle of a laser).

Building on John Stuart Mill's views, Cartwright conceives of abstract claims as being generic statements referring to the capacities of things to bring about certain empirical states of affairs by virtue of their natures. An important point is that capacity statements treat causes singly, and hence refer to "pure cases." In empirical reality, however, we mostly find mixed cases in which two or more causal capacities interfere. For this reason, theory construction—that is, in Cartwright's view, the hypothesizing and testing of separate capacity claims—requires us to abstract a pure case from a much more complex empirical situation. Conversely, in applying the theory to empirical reality we have to "add back all the causes that have been left out and calculate the total effect by combining the capacities" (Cartwright 1989, 185). In the case of lasers, the causal claims that have to be added in again may, for instance, include statements about absorption processes and about temperature. To avoid arbitrariness, the added causal factors should themselves be, or be based on, testable capacities.

To support the claim that theoretical science works by way of abstraction and to explain the process of abstraction, Cartwright puts forward several arguments. She distinguishes between symbolic representations and abstractions. The former are exemplified by idealizations, primarily those of a mathematical kind. Thus to conceive of the sun as a geometrically perfect sphere is to apply a mathematical idealization, because in fact the solar surface is quite irregular. Cartwright (1989, 187–88) argues that abstraction, though closely related, is still distinct from idealization.[3]

Regarding abstraction, she favors the following, Aristotelian interpretation. "I should like to reserve the word 'abstraction' to pick out a more Aristotelian notion, where 'abstraction' means 'taking away' or 'subtraction.' For Aristotle we begin with a concrete particular complete with all its properties. We then strip away—in our imagination—all that is irrelevant to the concerns of the moment to focus on some single property or set of properties, 'as if they were separate'" (Cartwright 1989, 197).

The cases of the relation between the concepts of work or coulomb force, on the one hand, and their concrete instances, on the other, are said to be paradigm examples of the idea of Aristotelian abstraction. The same applies to the relation between the claims about aspirin or lasers and their concrete instantiations. Cartwright explains the relationship between concrete and abstract concepts or claims from ordinary life as analogous to the connection between a (concrete) fable and its (abstract) moral. And she argues that the relation between abstract and concrete concepts or claims in science is (like) that between a general truth and a specific or local model for that truth.

In her interpretation of the ontological status of concepts, Cartwright again follows Aristotle, and she criticizes Platonic accounts of universals. Thus with respect to the concept of force she writes, "On my account *force* is to be regarded as an abstract concept. It exists only in the more specific forms to which it is led back via models. . . . It is not a new, separate property, different from any of the arrangements which exhibit it" (1999, 44). In the case of force, those more specific forms are the concrete arrangements of positions, extensions, motions, and masses of the particular bodies. More generally, Cartwright approvingly quotes Gotthold Lessing's claim that the general exists only in the particular.

Aristotelian Abstraction and Extensible Concepts

Cartwright's Aristotelian account of abstraction constitutes a variety of the classical doctrine of abstraction discussed and criticized in chapter 10. This doctrine, conceived as a method of acquiring concepts or forming theories, is untenable because of the fact that concepts and theories structure (our experiences of) the world. Construction of novel scientific concepts or theories cannot proceed by way of abstraction from the irrelevant properties of particulars. Cartwright (1999, 70–73) argues that, for empiricists, it is only the facts that make scientific statements true, and she claims that capacity statements can be supported by facts. What is entirely missing—probably because of those same empiricist premises—is a systematic treatment of the issue of how concepts structure those facts and of the philosophical implications of this structuring.

There is a further difference between the Aristotelian interpretation of abstraction and the one developed in the preceding chapters. It can be best explained with the help of the notions of leaving out and setting apart. While both interpretations include a similar idea of leaving out, they differ in the way they employ the notion of setting apart. According to the Aristotelian interpretation, the setting apart is only imagined, a mere focusing on properties as if they were separate. In my account, however, abstraction makes sense only in the context of the practice of extending concepts to novel situations. Remember the proposed replication of the original thoburve-raig experiment in the new context of the blind people. Clearly, this kind of extensibility assumes the possibility of a real separation in actual practice, over and above an imagined separation in thought.

Cartwright (1989, 202–6) develops her views through a discussion of the method of abstraction and concretization as proposed by Leszek Nowak (1980).[4] According to this method, a scientific investigation of the deep structure of the empirical phenomena involves two types of processes. First, by successively leaving out all secondary or nonessential factors, scientists are able to formulate abstract laws about the essence of the phenomena. Next, these laws can be tested in, and applied to, empirical reality by means of a process of concretization. This process requires us to systematically add back the secondary, or "corrective," factors. In her book *Nature's capacities and their measurement* (1989, 204), Cartwright takes Nowak's views on the relation between abstract and concrete to be right "in its basic outline," and she subscribes to his claim that the method of abstraction and concretization is the principal method used throughout the sciences, whether natural or social.

The way these views of Nowak's have been incorporated within Cartwright's framework is questionable, however. First, Nowak's account does not square well with the notion of Aristotelian abstraction. According to his account, abstraction is possible only within a particular theoretical or ontological orientation. It is this orientation that tells us which type of factors that bear upon a specific domain of phenomena should be taken as primary or essential and which as secondary or corrective (1980, 198–201). Thus he appears to agree with the criticisms of the classical doctrine of abstraction discussed in chapter 10: Aristotelian abstraction cannot work because it presupposes a prior theoretical-ontological structuring of the phenomena in question.

A related problem is pointed out by Paul Humphreys (1995, 158–59). He argues that, if it is really the case that we obtain abstract claims by consciously leaving out a specific set of empirical features, then the inverse process of concretization would be straightforward enough. In fact, however, scientific practice shows that the application of a theory is not a matter of simply adding back familiar secondary factors. Rather, finding out which are the appropriate "secondary" factors constitutes a genuine, and often hard-won, discovery (compare with Tiles and Oberdiek 1995, chap. 4).

Furthermore, Nowak's theory of abstraction and concretization as inverse processes cannot account for the extension of concepts to completely new contexts. The critical point is that, in extending a concept to a substantially novel situation, we do not add back all the causes that have been left out in abstracting from the original realization context. On the contrary, because the new context differs from the original one, all kinds of new causes will have to be taken into account. In contrast to Nowak's method of abstraction and concretization, my account of abstraction and nonlocal meaning is able to explain why extending a concept (or an experimental result) to a new situation is a matter of doing new research rather than merely filling out a list of well-known corrections. This account of the role of abstraction in extending concepts to new situations emerged from a detailed analysis of the reproduction and reproducibility of scientific experiments (Radder 1988, chap. 3; 1992; 1993; 1996, chap. 2; 2002; 2003b). The important analogy is the one between the extensibility of a concept to a novel observational process and the replicability of an experimental result by means of a different experimental process. The latter, however, should be clearly distinguished from the reproducibility of an experimental process under a fixed theoretical interpretation. It is only in reproducing an entire experimental process that one has to "add back" the (theoretically) relevant causal factors that played a role in the original experiment.

Remarkably enough, in Cartwright's 1999 book *The dappled world* there is not a single mention of Nowak's work. Apparently, she has omitted this aspect from her account of scientific abstraction because it may suggest a theory-dominated view of science (see Bailer-Jones, forthcoming). In particular, she now seems to reject the claim that abstraction and concretization are simply two reverse and reversible processes (see Cartwright 1999, chap. 4). Moreover, while her account of how abstraction works is rather different from mine, her explanation of why we use abstract concepts and claims seems to be related. Thus with respect to abstract capacity claims she writes, "A . . . major argument for capacities concerned the exportability of information: we gather information in one set of circumstances but expect to use it in circumstances that are quite different" (Cartwright 1989, 227). This is indeed the basic purpose of forming and using abstractions. As we have seen, however, this purpose cannot be adequately understood on the basis of an Aristotelian account of how abstraction works in practice.

In concluding this chapter, I would like to make two further observations. In the preceding chapters I emphasize that abstraction is not restricted to theory construction in modern science, since the extension of concepts is a general feature of human practice. Extensible concepts employed in the most mundane everyday practices are no less abstract than those used in the most esoteric theoretical sciences. Cartwright's position on this issue is both different from and similar to mine. It is different in that, in her empiricist account, there are both abstract and concrete concepts. A related and very significant difference is that abstract and concrete are conceived as relative notions; indeed, Cartwright often uses the locutions "more concrete" and "more abstract" (see, for instance, Cartwright 1999, 39–40). However, there is also a similarity between the two accounts of abstraction. Although Cartwright's work deals primarily with abstraction as a method that applies specifically to scientific theorizing, she also argues that similar methods are being used in the case of ordinary concepts and ordinary language. Thus she claims that "abstract-tendency laws seem to work in much the same way as ordinary generic sentences, like 'Dogs bark,' or habituals, like 'John smokes,' and to create many of the same problems. In all three forms it is equally difficult to say what connection there is between individual cases and the more general truth they fall under" (1989, 199). Again, in her 1999 book (37–43), she emphasizes the parallels between abstract scientific concepts (such as force) and abstract ordinary concepts (such as work). Hence she does not intend her theory of abstract concepts and statements to be strictly limited to science.

Finally, Cartwright's approach involves a strong focus on methodological questions. In her earlier work, she deliberately avoided metaphysical issues about abstract entities (1989, 3, 198–99). In contrast, in her more recent work she does not eschew metaphysical topics and she is prepared to draw ontological morals from methodological analyses (see, for example, Cartwright 1999, chaps. 3, 4). Thus she provides an ontology of things in terms of their capacities, tendencies, and natures. I am sympathetic to her nonactualist approach to these issues, as may be clear from the brief discussion of the ontology of human-independent potentialities and contingent realizations in chapter 10. As I also explain there, however, my account of abstraction deals with a different subject. It aims at an ontology not of things in the material world but of the meaning of concepts and their linguistic expressions.

14

Bruno Latour's work contains many examples of successful and unsuccessful extensions of scientific knowledge claims to novel situations. According to his philosophical interpretation, such attempted extensions should be seen as the core of scientific practice. Heterogeneous "actor networks" and the "translation" of the results of the interactions within these networks constitute two basic notions of his account of "science in action" (Latour 1987). A result, such as a particular knowledge claim, has been translated when the original actor network that sustained it in the first place has been successfully extended to a new situation. Generally speaking, such a translation involves both a reinterpretation and a (literal) displacement of the result.[1] To describe the network interactions and the processes of translation in an adequate manner, both human and nonhuman actors need to be taken into account.

Without too much strain, my description of the realization and interpretation of observational processes may be redescribed as the construction of heterogeneous actor networks, while the extension of concepts may be read as their translation from one type of process to another. Consider Koningsveld's experiment and its suggested replication in the case of the blind students. Clearly, the performance of the former experiment may be conceived as the construction of a complex network in which both human actors (for example, the students) and nonhuman actors (for instance, the sheets of paper) have been enrolled by the teacher with a view to strengthen the thob-urve-raig network. Furthermore, the planned replication of this experiment may be seen as an attempt to translate claims about thob, urve, and raig entities from the original network to a new actor network that includes the blind students and the manufactured tangible forms. In this way, the account of the extension and extensibility of concepts can be used to evaluate some of the far-reaching philosophical claims that Latour makes on the basis of his analyses of actor networks and processes of translation.[2]

The Extension of Actor Networks

For this purpose, I first look in more detail at the account of translation processes and the philosophical conclusions drawn from it. The critical question is how the relationship between the original and the novel observational process, or actor network, is described. Latour's text contains a number of conflicting statements concerning this question. Roughly, two different lines of argument can be found.

Along the first line, it is claimed that, in processes of translation, the original and the new network are being "made the same." By way of example, Latour briefly discusses the extension of claims about an experimental scale model of a new dam (in a hydraulics laboratory at Delft University of Technology) to claims about a real dam to be built in the Rotterdam harbor. Consider the following statements about this case. "*Whatever* may happen in the full-scale space-time [of the Rotterdam harbor], the engineers will have *already seen it*. They will have become slowly acquainted with *all* the possibilities, rehearsing *each* scenario at leisure. . . . They have already made *all* possible blunders and mistakes, safely inside the wooden hall in Delft" (Latour 1987, 231–32, emphasis added).

If the scale model were to achieve such results, this would not be due to its abstract truth but rather to the fact that, in a concrete process of translation, the harbor and its scale model have been successfully transformed so as to become copies of each other. More generally, Latour interprets all successful scientific predictions as being in fact based on hindsight. "In the end the prediction is fulfilled but it was in effect a *retro-diction*, exactly like the foresight . . . on the future of Rotterdam harbour . . . was in effect *hindsight*. . . . The predictable character of technoscience is entirely dependent on its ability to spread networks further" (Latour 1987, 249–50). Thus this line of argumentation assumes the existence of a very strong connection between the original and the new situation: a successful translation is guaranteed in so far as the two situations have been made the same (see also Latour 1983).

However, a second and somewhat different line of argument can also be found in Latour's text. In a number of other passages, he seems to shrink away from the strong claims he has made so far. For instance, he now apparently realizes that Delft engineers do not possess the unlimited foresight ascribed to them in the above quotations. "There is no guarantee that the events of the Delft scale model will be mimicked by the Rotterdam harbour in the next century" (Latour 1987, 236).

More generally, he no longer insists on the full similarity of the original and the novel situations. "Every time a fact is verified and a machine runs, it means that the lab or shop conditions have been extended *in some way*" (Latour 1987, 250). Taken together, the two quotations suggest that this second line of argument does not represent a substantially different insight but should be seen as a watering down of the first line in view of the practical problems of making the two situations completely identical.

We may summarize the two lines of argument as follows. Latour's basic view is that every successful scientific foresight about the extended network is in fact a hindsight, in the sense that it can be fully explained on the basis of the knowledge of the original network obtained in the past.[3] In this view, predictive success is entirely dependent on making the original and the new situation either fully identical (the first line of argument) or at least as similar as possible (the second line of argument). Both versions of this view are highly questionable.

Of course, if the two situations were (and remained) literally identical, we could know the development of the second situation on the basis of the evolution of the first. The evident problem is that the original and the novel situations can never be made fully identical, and the evolution of the latter can never be completely foreseen on the basis of what has happened in the former. Hence the first line of argumentation is obviously inadequate. At best, it could represent a regulative ideal that should be approximated as closely as possible in actual practice. Which brings us to the second line of argumentation.

Thus let us take a charitable reading and assume that the second line of reasoning represents Latour's more mature point of view. In this case, trying to make the two situations as similar as possible—for instance, by making them similar in increasingly many respects—seems to make sense. Unfortunately, as soon as it is admitted that perfect identity is impossible, the equation of foresight and hindsight breaks down. Without full similarity the possibility of predictive failure will always remain, because of the potential occurrence of some dissimilarity that has a significant influence on the course of the second situation.

However this may be, Latour's theory has to contend with a further problem, which is more directly relevant to the issue of nonlocal meaning and abstraction. Suppose that we add some more charity and read Latour as saying that made the same means taken to be the same. Perhaps the statement that the conditions of the original context must be extended "in some way" (see the last of the above quotations) might be adduced to support this reading. The problem of this interpretation, however, is that in many practical cases it is abundantly clear to everyone involved that the two situations are significantly or even radically different. A prime example is the situation in which an experimental result is taken to be replicable by means of a quite different experimental process or in which a concept is taken to be extensible to a substantially dissimilar observational process. In such cases, the explicit goal is often to make the two processes as different as possible to ensure that the replication or extension will count as a substantially novel achievement within the relevant scientific community.[4] Hence a significant class of processes of extension does not fit Latour's translation account. In such processes, the meaning of "translatable" results cannot be explained on the basis of the local characteristics of the original actor networks only.[5]

From my perspective, Latour's mistake is that, in focusing on the reproducibility of the entire (observational or experimental) process, he neglects the possibility of experimental replication through substantially novel processes. The underlying reason for this mistake is that he models science too closely on technology.[6] In contrast, I argue that, in a well-defined sense, the meaning of replicable results and extensible concepts transcends the meaning of all the processes, or actor networks, through which they have been realized so far. It is precisely the abstractness of replicable results, extensible concepts, and nonlocals that marks the distinction between the conceptual-theoretical dimension of science and its technological dimension of material realization.

These conclusions may also be used to assess Latour's account of the demarcation between science and nonscience. Consider what Latour calls the quandary of the fact builder. Given science's central goal of producing hard and unquestionable facts, ambitious fact builders have to confront a basic problem (Latour 1987, 103–8). If other scientists don't take up—that is to say, read, cite, or use—their claimed facts, they will be left alone with weak and isolated claims. But if others do take up their claimed facts, they may transform them beyond recognition, thus making invisible the role of the fact builders as their primary authors.

In Latour's view, there are basically two solutions to this quandary. The first is to give up the ambition of producing hard and unquestionable facts. "The simplest way to spread a statement is to leave *a margin of negotiation* to each of the actors to transform it as he or she sees fit and to *adapt it* to local circumstances" (Latour 1987, 208).

The advantage of this kind of translation is that it makes it relatively easy to interest others, since they will have the opportunity to use the stated facts for their own purposes. The disadvantage of this procedure, from the perspective of the ambitious fact builder, is that it does not produce hard facts. Thus if one wants such facts, as scientists do according to Latour, one needs to seek another solution. "This other solution to the quandary . . . is the one chosen by people who are called scientists and engineers. They prefer to increase control and to decrease the margin of negotiation. Instead of enrolling others by letting them transform the statement, they try to force them to take up the claim as it is" (Latour 1987, 209).

In this way, Latour draws a sharp contrast between a nonscientific and a scientific approach. The point of my discussion is that it shows the inadequacy of this "demarcation criterion" for the case of science. Instances of replicating scientific experiments and extending scientific concepts more closely conform to the first solution of the quandary. After all, these cases exemplify a way of spreading statements that offers ample opportunity for "adaptation to local circumstances," while there is no point in "forcing" the original and the new situation to be as similar as possible. The conclusion must be that Latour's demarcation criterion is inadequate since it does not cover these frequently occurring cases of replication and extension. Apparently, in these cases science is a less power-driven and warlike enterprise than Latour wants us to believe (compare with Amsterdamska 1990).

Abstract Laws and Theories

These arguments can be extended to bear upon Latour's views of abstraction and (mathematical) laws and theories. Although my own account is restricted to concepts, what concepts, laws, and theories share is, precisely, a nonlocal meaning and abstractness. For this reason, it makes sense to compare Latour's views of the meaning of laws and theories with my account of the meaning of concepts.[7]

Latour's basic position on laws and theories, and their mathematical expressions, is that they fit the actor-network approach as well as the more empirical aspects of science do. A theoretical equation, such as Ohm's law, "is no different in nature from all the other tools that allow elements to be brought together, mobilised, arrayed and displayed; no different from a table, a questionnaire, a list, a graph, a collection" (Latour 1987, 238).

Moreover, laws and theories are not autonomous. In line with the empiricist tendency that characterizes Latour's work, he is at pains not to ascribe an autonomous meaning to abstract theories and equations. Their meaning cannot be established in abstraction of the networks (for instance, the setting up of a table or the filling out of a questionnaire) from which they have been derived. "The equations . . . constitute, literally, the *sum* of all these mobilisations, evaluations, tests and ties. They tell us what is associated with what" (Latour 1987, 240).

Thus laws and theories are merely a special kind of summary of more empirical results of science, and hence their meaning remains tied to the meaning of the various local networks, the results of which they summarize. Yet Latour emphasizes the basic significance of theoretical and mathematical work for (the study of) science. Mathematical theories are "the true heart" of scientific networks, and their observation, study, and interpretation is more important than that of the construction of facts (Latour 1987, 240–41).

Latour illustrates his views of the meaning of laws and theories with the case of Thomas Edison's construction of a system of electric lighting during the late 1870s and early 1880s. This large technological system was meant to be competitive with, and eventually to supplant, the system of gas lighting. A major part of the construction work was the invention of the incandescent lamp. Edison's invention resulted from a synthesis of economic, technological, and scientific aspects (Hughes 1979; see also Hughes 1983, chap. 2). On the one hand, in view of the high price of copper, the conductors needed to be as thin as possible to make the technology competitive. On the other hand, conductors with a large cross section are required if one wants to minimize energy losses through heat production during the distribution of the electricity. The combined laws of Ohm and Joule suggested a way out of this dilemma to Edison and his collaborators. These laws imply that increasing the resistance of the lamp filaments will keep the electric currents small, and hence the energy loss, even in thin conductors, will be limited. Thus the task was to find a high-resistance filament that also met the other technical requirements for use in an incandescent lamp, such as durability, infusibility, and the possibility of parallel wiring.

In this way, Edison's reasoning combined a theoretical-mathematical argument with economic and technological considerations. Led by results derived from the laws of Ohm and Joule, he started a systematic experimental search for an appropriate filament. Thomas Hughes (1979, 137) describes the episode as follows. "Edison stated that in the fall of 1878 he had experimented with carbon filaments but that the major problem with these was their low resistance. . . . An apparently remote consideration (the amount of copper used for conductors), was really the commercial crux of the problem. . . . Edison then said that he turned from carbon to various metals in order to obtain a filament of high resistance, continuing along these lines until about April 1879 when he had a platinum of great promise because the occluded gases had been driven out of it, thereby increasing its infusibility." Latour presents the case of Edison as supporting his actor-network approach in general and his "operationalist" interpretation of the meaning of theoretical concepts—such as those occurring in the laws of Ohm and Joule —in particular.

Edison's invention of the incandescent lamp does not suit Latour's framework, however, but instead confirms the significance of the nonlocality of the meaning of (scientific) concepts. To see this, consider the following account of the events. The concepts at issue were primarily the concepts from the nineteenth-century theories of electricity and heat, such as electric current, voltage, resistance, power, and energy. At the time Edison started his searches, these concepts had been realized in a number of particular experimental processes by Ohm and Joule, and they had been shown to be related in a specific manner. Edison's search for a high-resistance filament and his intention to experiment on "various metals," including platinum, was based on the assumption that the experiments of Ohm and Joule are replicable. That is to say, Edison's plans make sense only if he presupposed that Ohm's and Joule's experimental results might be replicated in the novel context of his own experiments. In other words, when Edison started his experimental search he assumed that the concepts in question (including their relationships) have a nonlocal meaning that transcends the meaning they had as a consequence of their use in the experiments by Ohm and Joule. In this respect, Edison's intention to search for a high-resistance filament proves to be comparable to the intention to replicate the thob-urve-raig experiment in the context of the blind people.

Edison searched for a new metal with specific properties. He did not try to make his experiments as similar as possible to those of Ohm and Joule. In a specific way, he severed the concepts and laws of Ohm and Joule from the networks in which they had been realized thus far. In other words, the implied claim about the nonlocality of the meaning of the relevant concepts and laws structured Edison's search process and guided him in a particular direction. The crucial point is that this structuring and guiding took place before the replications of the experiments of Ohm and Joule had been actually realized. Latour, in contrast, claims that theoretical laws and mathematical concepts or equations can make a difference only "once the networks are in place" (Latour 1987, 239). Hence he is unable to explain this important episode in Edison's construction of a system of electric lighting. The underlying reason for this shortcoming is that an interpretation of (theoretical) concepts and relationships as a mere sum of past actions cannot do justice to the future-oriented, heuristic significance of extensible concepts.[8]

MEANING FINITISM AND THE SOCIOLOGY OF SCIENTIFIC
KNOWLEDGE

The open-ended nature of the meaning of concepts has also been stressed by some authors within the sociology of scientific knowledge. It is instructive to point out some agreements and disagreements between their views and the ones proposed here. Barry Barnes, David Bloor, and John Henry advocate what they call a sociological, finitist account of the meaning of concepts, in particular those concepts that attempt to classify "natural kinds." They write, "The future applications of terms are open-ended. This is merely a reformulation of the central tenet of finitism. On a finitist account there is nothing identifiable as 'the meaning' of a kind term, no specification or template or algorithm fully formed in the present, capable of fixing the future correct use of the term, of distinguishing in advance all the things to which it will eventually be correctly applicable" (1996, 55).

Their book *Scientific knowledge* (1996) provides a comprehensive review of the influential "interest approach" developed by Barnes and Bloor, in particular, since about the mid-1970s. The focus of the book is on scientific knowledge, but the theoretical position adopted by its authors is meant to apply to any kind of knowledge. Moreover, in spite of its subtitle—*A sociological analysis*—the book largely deals with philosophical assumptions and implications of the sociology of (scientific) knowledge. Although the authors extend their finitist account of concepts to beliefs and theories, I address here only what they say about concepts.

Barnes, Bloor, and Henry support their claims about concepts and their meaning by means of a general philosophical argument (see also Hesse 1974; Barnes 1983; Bloor 1996). Briefly, it goes like this. Forming a concept by classifying a group of particulars into a class relies not on a strict identity of its members but on certain similarities between these members. Since "similarity" always amounts to "similarity in a certain respect," all members of the class will exhibit certain dissimilarities as well. Hence, when we are confronted with a potentially new instance of the concept, it is a matter of contingent judgment whether we will or will not deem the similarities more important than the dissimilarities. Thus identifying a new case as a member of the class requires taking a decision. Barnes, Bloor, and Henry call this the problem of the next case. Because the argument is taken to apply to any concept whatsoever, the problem of the next case is uneliminable. Facing it can be postponed by moving to more explicit and stricter definitions of the class, but ultimately the problem cannot be avoided. Neither can it be definitely solved, in a strictly logical sense. For this reason, Barnes, Bloor, and Henry (1996, 56–57) conclude that "no act of classification is ever indefeasibly correct" and hence "all acts of classification are revisable."

This does not mean, though, that our concepts are continually changing. Barnes, Bloor, and Henry go on to argue that, in practice, the criteria for what counts as correctly using a concept are fixed by the prevailing goals and interests of particular traditions and cultures. It is here that they see the point of a sociological analysis of scientific knowledge. "The suggestion is then that goals and interests are associated with scientific research in all actual situations, and operate as contributory causes of the actions or series of actions which constitute the research. The causes help to solve the problem of the next case, of why a term is applied or an exemplar extended in that particular way that time" (1996, 120).[1]

To support these claims, Barnes, Bloor, and Henry (1996, 121–24) cite and discuss Henk van den Belt's study of a nineteenth-century controversy concerning the classification of certain chemical substances (1989). The controversy occurred in France, between 1860 and 1863. At issue was whether or not certain varieties of red dyes (the so-called aniline reds) were all of the same kind. On the one hand, contemporary academic chemistry classified all aniline reds as salts of rosaniline. Hence they were identified by most chemists as being "essentially" the same. On the other hand, for the purpose of practical, industrial dye production, these substances were recognized as clearly different. The latter position could also be, and was in fact, supported by chemical experts. After all, in addition to their similarities, the aniline reds also exhibited certain chemical dissimilarities. The question was brought to court, because one dye manufacturer claimed that the patent granted to him for one variety of aniline red effectively applied to all varieties. To support the assertion that all aniline reds were essentially the same, this manufacturer and his lawyers appealed to the research of the chemist A. W. Hofmann. His competitors, however, assisted by their own chemical experts, contested this assertion. Eventually, the court decided in favor of the identity claim.

Since they take both the identity claim and the difference claim as being in themselves reasonable, Barnes, Bloor, and Henry conclude that the decision by the court could not be based on inspection of the "purely intrinsic" qualities of the aniline reds. Instead, it resulted from the clash between the goals and interests of the parties involved (primarily, the dye manufacturers, their lawyers, the chemists, and the judges). Thus it was the prevailing interests and goals that fixed, for about one decade, what counted as the correct criteria for classifying aniline reds. During that period, those criteria were routinely applied to solve new problems of a next case of classifying certain red dyes.

Finite or Nonlocal Meanings?

How does this theory of meaning finitism relate to the view that concepts both structure the world and abstract from it? The claim that concepts structure the world seems to be implied by, or can be quite easily incorporated within, meaning finitism. After all, the finitist account of the meaning and use of concepts proposed by Barnes, Bloor, and Henry is, in at least some important respects, similar to Herman Koningsveld's account. Consider, for example, a new performance of the thob-urve-raig experiment as discussed in chapter 8. It might well be that, for purely contingent reasons, the interest in thob, urve, and raig things is fading away. At the same time, the classification in terms of Greek characters, Roman characters, and logical or mathematical symbols might come to be seen as the correct one, even if this were to entail that a few of the figures need to be considered as anomalies or noise. The possibility of this alternative interpretation shows that the criterion for what counts as the correct classification cannot be derived from inherent properties of the entities themselves. In agreement with finitism, the thob, urve, and raig classification proves to be essentially revisable, and concrete revisions will depend on the changing interests and goals associated with those involved in performing the experiment.[2]

There is a further similarity between the sociological account of the meaning of concepts and the view that concepts both structure the world and abstract from it. Within the approach advocated by Barnes, Bloor, and Henry, it is, strictly speaking, improper to talk about the meaning of concepts or words as such, outside their contexts of use. They emphasize that concepts and words, in contrast to the goals and interests they mediate, possess no intrinsic causal powers. Ultimately, it is not the meanings of concepts or words but the underlying goals and interests that make particular usages correct or incorrect. Thus, according to sociological finitism, the claim that concepts structure the world needs to be qualified. It is the uses of concepts, rather than the concepts themselves, that structure the world.

Similarly, my account of the structuring and abstracting meaning components of concepts goes beyond the level of pure concepts and their linguistic expressions. As we have seen, both components imply a relation between the concept and a set of observational processes. The structuring meaning component depends on the past and present realization of a set of observational processes, while the abstracting meaning component—that is to say, the nonlocal meaning of the concept—depends on an indeterminate set of potentially realizable observational processes. In this specific way, I subscribe to the point of Barnes, Bloor, and Henry. A cogent account of the meaning of concepts should not be limited to their verbal expressions but should also address their (actual or possible) realization in observational processes.

In spite of these similarities, there also is a basic disagreement between finitism and the theory of the nonlocality of meaning. This disagreement derives from the fact that in using concepts we not only structure the world but also abstract from it. According to the finitist doctrine, the meaning of a concept at a particular moment is determined by the class of its then-accepted instances. "A class is its accepted instances at a given point in time: those instances are the existing resources for deciding what else belongs in the class, the available precedents for further acts of classification, the basis for further case-to-case development of the classification" (Barnes, Bloor, and Henry 1996, 105, my emphasis).

Extensible concepts, however, possess a nonlocal meaning component. Because of this, the meaning of such concepts transcends the meaning of the set of particular processes in which they have been realized so far. Furthermore, the intended extension of concepts to basically different contexts entails a specific dynamics of concept formation and articulation that does not primarily draw on the set of accepted instances. Hence, this dynamics differs from the way classificatory concepts are assumed to develop according to Barnes, Bloor, and Henry.

Self-Reference and Infinite Regress

Clearly, finitism constitutes a direct challenge to the view that concepts abstract from the world and hence possess a nonlocal meaning. This challenge can be met, however, by demonstrating the implausibility of core assumptions of sociological meaning finitism. I do so by offering two arguments. The first shows that finitism suffers from a problem of self-reference. On the one hand, sociologists of scientific knowledge interpret their approach as a naturalistic enterprise. Drawing a fundamental methodological boundary between the natural and the human sciences is claimed to be improper, and hence the sociological study of science can and should itself be practiced scientifically.[3] Barnes, Bloor, and Henry take this to imply that the principal method of the sociology of scientific knowledge is the presentation and analysis of historical—and, more generally, empirical—case studies.

On the other hand, the central tenets of the theory of meaning finitism are advanced as being completely general, as applying to any use of concepts whatsoever. Hence they should also apply to the future uses of the concept of meaning finiteness. But what is the evidence for the latter claim? In line with the naturalistic case study approach, the evidence consists of a number of past instances of meaning finiteness of concepts, primarily taken from the history of science. That is to say, Barnes, Bloor, and Henry conclude from a number of past instances of meaning finiteness of concepts that the meaning of all future instances of concepts will be finite. But this conclusion flatly contradicts the theory of meaning finitism. After all, this theory tells us that past applications of a term (in this case, the term "meaning finiteness") do not fix future applications. That is to say, it is the theory of finitism itself that prevents the step from the case studies of finite meanings to the general doctrine of finitism.[4]

In addition to this problem of self-reference, there is a second and, I think, more serious problem. The alleged sociological solution of the problem of the next case leads to an infinite regress, and hence the sociology of scientific knowledge cannot have the explanatory power ascribed to it by its proponents. Barnes, Bloor, and Henry (1996, 78–79) point out that finitism is a formal claim. It says that past and present meanings and uses of concepts do not logically determine future meanings and uses. This formal claim is held to be compatible with the empirical fact that frequently people feel compelled to extend concepts in a fixed manner. Thus finitism denies logical compulsion, but it allows for psychological or social compulsion. The latter, it is claimed, can be explained by the sociological analysis of scientific knowledge. In their explanans, Barnes, Bloor, and Henry make essential use of the concepts of "goal" and "interest." They argue that the empirical fact that conceptual practice is often strongly constrained can be explained by taking into account the persistence of psychological and social goals and interests. More precisely, in the case of a new, potential instance of a term, it is the social interests and goals that prevail in the relevant tradition or culture that help to explain why the term is being extended in a particular way.

Finitism claims to offer a general theory of the meaning of concepts, which also applies to the concepts of the sociology of scientific knowledge. "If sociologists are to uncover *general* principles at work in the production of knowledge, these principles will inform their own attempts to detect, formulate, illustrate and justify those very principles. If they did not, then the sociology of knowledge would be in danger of demonstrating its own falsity" (Barnes, Bloor, and Henry 1996, 45).

However, this reflexive approach leads to an infinite regress when applied to the subject of sociological explanation. Consider a case in which some object x has been classified by a scientist on the basis of concept C. Next, a second scientist applies the same concept C to some other object x', which is thus taken to be similar to x. The sociological explanation of these corresponding acts of classification will refer to a common set of goals and interests. In particular, it will claim that the concept $G\&I$, that is to say, "being affected by the specific goal G and the specific interest I," applies to the two scientists. Now, suppose that a third scientist classifies a further object x'' as also being C. A sociological explanation of the latter act of classification would have to assume that the concept $G\&I$ may be extended to the case of this third scientist. Since this assumption cannot be justified by inspecting the intrinsic qualities of the three scientists, the sociological explanation is itself confronted with the problem of the next case. Thus the sociological explanans becomes itself an explanandum.

One way to solve the sociological problem of the next case is to move to the higher level of the sociology of the sociology of scientific knowledge and introduce specific metagoals and meta-interests.[5] But of course, this move will not help either, since the same problem will return at this metasociological level. Thus the proposed solution of the problem of the next case leads to an infinite explanatory regress: suppose we want to explain why a problem of the next case in science or ordinary life is solved in one way or another; this presupposes the solution of a problem of the next case in the sociology of science, but solving the latter problem requires the solution of a problem of the next case at the metasociological level, and so on ad infinitum. Hence the attempt to explain the finite meaning of a particular concept constitutes an infinite sociological research project.

In sum, the sociological theory of meaning finitism suffers from two serious problems. First, if the meanings of all concepts—including the concept of finitism—are finite, finitism cannot be the general theory that it claims to be. Second, the sociological approach to the problem of the next case leads to an infinite explanatory regress. For this reason, the sociology of (scientific) knowledge is unable to provide an adequate explanatory account of the empirical constraints that limit the changeability of concepts. Because of these two problems, the sociological theory of meaning finitism does not constitute a viable alternative to the view that extensible concepts possess a nonlocal meaning.

The underlying problem is that Barnes, Bloor, and Henry do not distinguish between ontological and (social) epistemological issues. The ontological conclusion from the discussion in chapters 9 and 10 is that, if a concept is extensible, it has a nonlocal meaning that transcends the meaning of its past and present realizations. Surely it is a contingent empirical question whether concepts can and will actually be extended and how far their extensions will range in space and time. Thus, regarding the social epistemological issue, I agree with Barnes, Bloor, and Henry. For instance, the fact that Koningsveld's original experiment proves to be successful in classifying the entities in question as being thob, urve, or raig does not guarantee the success of its replication with the blind students. Yet the frequent successes of conceptual extensions imply that the notion of extensible concepts, and hence the ontological notion of nonlocal meanings, makes sense; these successes also show that the claim that a concept is extensible and has a nonlocal meaning can be empirically confirmed, even if it will necessarily remain a fallible claim. Thus, regarding the ontological issue, my approach clearly differs from the views of the proponents of meaning finitism.

Meaning and Use

The finitists follow Ludwig Wittgenstein's slogan that meaning is use. As Bloor puts it, "Meaning follows usage, and so cannot exist ahead of it to guide it or to act as an independent reality against which to measure usage" (1996, 850). In contrast, I argue that meaning cannot be reduced to (past and present) use. The basic reason for this is that extensible concepts not only structure but also abstract from our past and present world.

My critique of sociological meaning finitism holds not only for the interest approach to the sociology of scientific knowledge but also in the case of other broadly social constructivist accounts of science. Thus Harry Collins's account of formalization and digitization (1990, chaps. 2, 4), which I briefly discuss in chapter 12, is quite similar to the Barnes, Bloor, and Henry approach. It adds to this approach a sociological account of the use of discrete concepts.[6] More generally, Collins endorses the finitist identification of meaning and use: "the meaning of something equals its use in a form of life" (Collins and Yearley 1992, 308, note 9). For this reason, the critique of meaning finitism also applies to Collins's interpretation of the meaning of digitized concepts. An analogous conclusion holds for Michael Lynch's ethnomethodological appropriation of Wittgenstein's later philosophy. After all, in Lynch's view the relationship between linguistic meaning and local practices is even tighter than it is in the sociological approach of Barnes, Bloor, and Henry (see Lynch 1992; Bloor 1992).

The question of whether or not my critique applies to the later Wittgenstein himself is harder to decide. Instead of embarking on an endless exegesis of Wittgenstein's work, I offer a mere registration of the views of two commentators. According to Ilkka Niiniluoto, "If linguistic meaning is identified with 'use' following Wittgenstein's suggestion, . . . it should not be understood as the sum of actual uses only, but its possible or potential uses should be included as well" (1999, 85).

In contrast, Herbert Marcuse sharply criticizes Wittgenstein's later ordinary language philosophy for its one-dimensional affirmation of actual usage. "Thinking (or at least its expression) is not only pressed into the straitjacket of common usage, but also enjoined not to ask and seek solutions beyond those that are already there. . . . The self-styled poverty of philosophy, committed with all its concepts to the given state of affairs, distrusts the possibilities of a new experience" (1968, 144). Thus, while Niiniluoto suggests that the notion of potential use follows Wittgenstein's lead, Marcuse ascribes to Wittgenstein the view that the explication of the meaning of concepts can, and should, terminate in the actual universe of ordinary discourse.

PRODUCT PATENTING AS THE EXPLOITATION OF ABSTRACT POSSIBILITIES

Thus far, the question of how concepts structure the world and abstract from it is addressed as follows. Chapters 8 through 11 provide the basic answer to this question and thus constitute the core of part 2 of this book. Next, chapters 12 through 15 develop the account of abstraction and the nonlocal meaning of concepts by means of a critical discussion of several alternative views on the issues in question. These other views—regarding formalization, Aristotelian abstraction, extension of actor networks, and meaning finitism—are of a quite general philosophical nature. Hence the relevant chapters aim to position my account of abstraction and nonlocal meaning with respect to these philosophical alternatives.

In this chapter, I develop this account of abstraction and nonlocal meaning in a somewhat different direction, namely, by applying it to a particular problem concerning the patenting of scientific and technological inventions. The focus is on a specific type of patents, the so-called product patents, which have gained a strongly increased significance during the past two decades. Recently, the issue of patenting has been much debated, in particular as a consequence of rapid developments in biotechnology and genomics. Many patents, including product patents, have been granted for particular genes of plants, animals, and humans and for (parts of) plants and animals. Thus in the 1990s the U.S. biotechnology firm Agracetus acquired two patents on major agricultural products: one for all genetically modified cotton, for any trait and for any method of modification, and a similar one for all genetically manipulated soybeans (Shulman 1999, 91–102).

The main claim of this chapter is that the idea of a product patent is basically flawed. Interestingly enough, this claim proves to be an immediate corollary of my account of extensible concepts. In fact, the product that is being patented is not a concrete technological invention but rather an abstract conceptual possibility in the sense discussed in the preceding chapters. Hence, since current patent laws exclude the patentability of concepts, product patents should not be granted at all. To enable a better appreciation of the meaning and scope of this conclusion, I first offer some explanation of what is at issue in present-day patenting practices in science and technology.

The Theory and Practice of Patenting

The official goal of the patent system is to protect a particular type of intellectual property, namely, technological inventions. A patent grants to its holder the exclusive right to turn the invention into money, provided that its exploitation does not contradict any law or legal regulations. Thus the patent holder is entitled to commercially exploit the invention and to prevent others from making, using, or selling it. The legal protection is restricted in time, usually for a period of twenty years. Holding a patent offers industry the opportunity to regain the investments made for realizing the invention.

The term "industry," by the way, must be interpreted broadly: it includes the research carried out in our "entrepreneurial" universities. The strong commercialization of science has entailed an increasing number of patent applications and grants by academic researchers and institutions. In the United States universities are legally obliged to patent and commercialize the intellectual property that results from federally sponsored research. In Europe comparable measures to the same effect have been taken.[1] We should bear in mind, though, that what is patentable is the technological invention as a type of human-made, material thing or process. Even if the technological invention is largely or fully based on theoretical, scientific knowledge, according to official doctrine, knowledge as such cannot be patented.

To be patentable, inventions need to satisfy the criteria of novelty, nonobviousness, and utility.[2] In the context of patent law, an invention is novel if it does not form part of the current state of the art, and it is nonobvious if, according to the skilled expert, it involves a genuine technical achievement. In return for being granted a patent, the invention must be "disclosed" through submitting a publicly accessible description of the invention to the relevant patent office. This description should enable the patent office to examine whether the invention is really novel, nonobvious, and usable. Moreover, the public disclosure of the description entails that other companies or universities do not need to waste time and money by reinventing the same wheel. Patents may be granted for processes, for products, or for both processes and their products. In the case of a product patent, the rights apply to the product as such. That is to say, even if the product were brought about through a process that differs substantially or completely from the one originally used by the inventor, the rights of the patentee would still hold.

All this might look relatively straightforward. In practice, however, applying for a patent, having it granted, and maintaining it against litigation is rather complicated (see, for example, Sterckx 2000a). Many issues of a scientific, technological, legal, moral, or even philosophical nature may, and often do, arise.

First, as we have seen, the applicant for a patent needs to disclose the invention by means of a publicly accessible description. This description should make it possible for a skilled colleague to reproduce the invention. In this context, the question may arise of whether the account of the invention is sufficiently detailed so as to enable this reproduction.

Furthermore, the aim of a patent is to protect the intellectual property of individuals or individual institutions. Hence it must be established that the applicant is the rightful owner of the intellectual property in question. Since scientific and technological inventions often result from collective work, both practical and more principled questions may be posed about the issue of individual ownership. Consider, for example, the Agracetus patent on soybeans, mentioned at the beginning of this chapter. This patent was based on a so-called gene gun method. As was openly admitted by one of the inventors, this method refined and extended an earlier version of a gene gun developed by another group of researchers. In this case, the competing claims were settled privately by the parties involved (see Shulman 1999, 93–95).

Next, in patent law a distinction is made between inventions and discoveries. Technological inventions of artificially constructed processes and products are patentable, while scientific discoveries of naturally occurring phenomena are not. Thus it is important to answer the question of whether the application bears on a technological invention or on a discovery of a natural phenomenon. This question is particularly delicate in the case of claimed patents on genes or other parts of living organisms. To patent a gene or another part of an organism, a scientist needs to isolate it from its natural state and identify an industrially useful property for it. In such cases, it has been debated whether or not the gene or the part of the organism itself—in contrast to the technological process through which it has been isolated—may count as a human-made artifact.

Resolving such issues presupposes, at least roughly, a philosophical conception of science and technology, including their mutual similarities and dissimilarities. Different philosophical interpretations—for instance, constructivism and realism—can be expected to lead to different views of what is an invention and what a discovery. Thus the editors of an influential volume on the social construction of technological systems make the following claim. "In the social constructivist approach, the key point is not that the social is given any special status behind the natural; rather, it is claimed that there is nothing but the social: socially constructed natural phenomena, socially constructed social interests, socially constructed artifacts, and so on" (Bijker, Hughes, and Pinch 1987, 109).

Clearly, in such a strictly constructivist account, all natural phenomena studied by science are artificial (social) constructs. Hence, if the constructions satisfy the other criteria, they are all patentable. At the other extreme, Steven Luper (1999) denies the relevance of the distinction between inventions and discoveries. From his realist perspective, inventions of types of processes or products are actually discoveries of something that was there all along. Types of gadgets and life forms, for instance, are claimed to be quite similar to sunlight and laws of nature. Hence, under the present system of patent laws and regulations, "inventions" of such types of gadgets and life forms should not be patentable.

Furthermore, even after a patent has been granted, problems may arise in maintaining it. The patent holder may claim the applicability of the patent to a certain product or process manufactured by others, but this claim may be contested by the other party by arguing that the product or process in question is not really the same as the original one. In my discussion of meaning finitism and the sociology of scientific knowledge, in the preceding chapter, I briefly review a case study of such a controversy, which took place in France in the 1860s. In this case, the patentee claimed that a new variety of dye was chemically similar to the one covered by his patent. This claim was contested in court on the grounds that, in terms of practical, industrial production processes, the original and the new varieties of aniline red differed considerably (see Van den Belt 1989).

Finally, there are significant differences between countries. Patent law has, in the first instance, a national scope. Thus in the United States almost everything is patentable, as long as it satisfies the criteria of novelty, nonobviousness, and utility. European patent law tends to be somewhat less liberal. There is, for example, a general rule that excludes inventions that go against the "public order" or "morality" from being patentable. An example would be an invention that, if implemented, would cause unnecessary suffering by animals without any compensating benefits. Also, parts of the human body cannot be patented (unless they are isolated from the body by means of a technological process). Clearly, the motive for such rules is primarily social and ethical. It is the case, though, that the European Union—under pressure from the biotechnology industry and from the U.S. government—tends to move toward the U.S. model. It does so by attempting to restrict the number of exclusions of patentability and by interpreting the allowed exclusions as narrowly as possible (see Sterckx 2000c).

Broad Patents and Product Patents

Clearly, a comprehensive discussion of the actual practice and the normative desirability of patenting may easily expand into a book-length work. I focus here on one issue, namely, the issue of the legitimacy of the concept and practice of product patenting.

The crucial point is the distinction, made in patent applications, between the specification of the invention and the claims of the patent. On the basis of this distinction the inventor needs to describe (at least) one specific process through which the product can be produced, but the claimed patent may go far beyond the invention as embodied in this specific process. In most cases, patent applications contain a series of claims of different scope. As one applicant stated, "If you have a good patent agent, the first claim of most patents will always be that you claim half the world, and then you try to trim down" (Sterckx 2000b, 371).[3]

Thus in the 1980s researchers at Harvard University isolated a gene that, when built into the genome of a certain kind of mice, increases their probability of getting cancer. Because such a genetically modified mouse can be used in cancer research (for example, to test the efficacy of drugs), the invention had potential utility. Since it also satisfied the criteria of novelty and nonobviousness, a U.S. patent for this so-called oncomouse was granted to Harvard University in 1988. The oncomouse patent contains twelve claims, the last of which bears upon the actually modified mice. The first, however, claims the exploitation of the invention for *all transgenic, nonhuman, mammalian onco-animals*. The patent has been granted in spite of the fact that no proof was submitted of either the actual technological feasibility of applying the method to animals other than mice or the carcinogenic effects of the oncogene in those animals. In recent years, many of these so-called broad patents have been granted.[4]

In spite of this, product patents go one critical step further. In the case of broad patents, some of the other processes through which a product might be obtained are at least hinted at. A product patent, however, once it has been granted, is valid for any known or unknown process in which the product plays a relevant role. In this sense, product patents can be seen to be a limiting case of broad patents. Product patents are obviously extremely broad, but not all broad patents are also product patents.

Product patents are particularly relevant to the patenting of genetically modified organisms. In these cases, the patents are claimed to apply not merely to the actually modified organisms but also to their offspring. In her discussion of the legal and ethical dimensions of biotechnology patents in Europe, Geertrui van Overwalle summarizes the issue as follows.

The problem of reproducibility of biological inventions has, like a Sisyphean rock, rolled back and forth over the years. But the German Bundesgerichtshof finally decided that the strict reproducibility requirement as such—by which I mean the repetition of the process of making—would only apply to *process* protection for the end product, but that in order for *product* protection to be granted for a new organism as such, the repetition of the process of making was not necessary, and the deposit of the new micro-organism together with the description of the multiplication method would suffice. Transferring the jurisprudence of the German Supreme Court to plants would signify that *product* protection for plants is always possible, because the most important dogmatic impediment to patenting plants, namely the repetition of the process of making, is removed. (2000, 204)

That is to say, product patent claims on a genetically modified organism remain valid for its offspring, even if this offspring is not generated through technological laboratory processes but through a natural process of reproduction. It will be clear that the existence of such patents may have a huge impact on traditional farming practices. For one thing, farmers who sow patented seeds are no longer free to use or sell the seeds resulting from their own harvest, as they used to do in the past (see Shulman 1999, 83–91).

Apparently, both patent applicants and patent offices see the distinction between specification and claim, as well as the procedure of product patenting based on it, as appropriate and justified. Even more, during the past two decades there has been a shift from process to product patenting in many countries. The economic reasons for this shift are obvious. The product patent offers better chances for more and unexpected profits, and it can be defended more easily against possible litigation. But there are two further reasons for this shift toward product patenting. The first has to do with the increased significance of science, particularly theoretical science, for technology. In many cases, the distinction between the specification of the invention and the claim of the patent will derive from the differentiation between the material realization of experiments and the theoretically claimed significance of their results. The second reason for the rise of product patents has to do with the large growth of patent applications in the areas of biology and medicine. In these areas, moral reasons often prevent immediate experimenting on humans. Hence potential diagnostic methods or drugs are first tried out on experimental animals. Ultimately, however, the invested money should be returned from methods and drugs for humans. Thus biomedical industries are naturally led to extrapolate their inventions toward the human domain. That is to say, to control their eventual market they will tend to go for broad patents and product patents.

Three Arguments against Product Patenting

The practice of issuing broad patents has not gone unchallenged. This practice has been debated and questioned from a variety of perspectives, and in a number of legal cases the original patent claims have been rescinded.[5] Thus, after many years of protracted legal and political procedures, the Canadian Supreme Court recently rejected the oncomouse patent. My approach joins these critical voices, but its focus and line of argumentation are different. I focus on product patents and demonstrate their problematic nature by developing three distinct arguments. The second and third arguments rely on my account of the reproducibility of experiments or technologies and on my analysis of the relationship between replicable experimental or technological results and extensible concepts.

My first argument against product patenting arises from a general principle that is often claimed to justify the existence of the patent system as such. The principle says that the system promotes socially desirable innovation because it stimulates competitors to develop alternatives to the patented inventions. In the case of product patents, however, the validity of this argument is doubtful. Suppose that a certain product is seen as socially desirable, but that its production process has a number of obvious disadvantages. For instance, this process may not be optimally efficient, safe, or environmentally friendly. If a patent is granted for this product, competitors will not be free to manufacture and market the product with clearly improved production processes. Thus in such cases product patents hamper rather than promote socially desirable innovation. As pointed out by Henk van den Belt (pers. comm.), this objection to product patenting has played a substantial role in history. In 1877, a similar argument was put forward by the German Chemical Society in a critique of a newly proposed patent law. As a result, product patents in the areas of chemistry and pharmacy (in German, *Stoffpatente*) were prohibited in Germany until 1967. We may conclude from this first argument that product patenting is questionable in the light of a major principle underlying the patent system as such.

Product Patenting as the Exploitation of Abstract Possibilities

My second argument against product patenting composes the core of my critique. It addresses the issue of the adequacy of the technical specification of the invention. This specification must be such that, in principle, it enables an experienced scientist or technologist to copy the invention and to check its operation. That is to say, the invention must be reproducible by the members of the inventor's peer group.[6]

In the practice of science and technology, however, different types of reproducibility can be found, two of which are pertinent here (see Radder 1996, chaps. 2, 4; see also chaps. 9, 10, and 14, above). First, there is the reproducibility of the entire experimental or technological process leading to a particular product (or result, as I have called it thus far). Consider, for example, the ruby laser that produces a narrow, intensive, and coherent light ray—a laser beam—by means of the excitation of chromium atoms in a ruby crystal. A theoretical specification of the processes taking place in a ruby laser may enable their reproducibility by skilled experimenters.

In addition, reproducibility may apply to the product or result of experimental or technological processes, independent of the way(s) in which that product has so far been realized in practice. This second type of reproducibility is also called replicability. The first operating laser, the ruby laser, was built in 1960. In the next two decades, many different types of lasers were constructed, using various lasing materials and embodying quite different technologies: gas lasers, free-electron lasers, X-ray lasers, and so on (Hecht 1987, 577–93; De Ruiter 1992, chap. 3). Yet in 1960, the statement "that laser beams are replicable through quite different processes" was no more than a claim. It indicated a possibility, not a fact. To know whether or not that possibility could be realized, much detailed theoretical and experimental research still needed to be done.

The distinction between these two types of reproducibility is relevant to the issue of product patenting. The practice of science and technology shows that the reproducibility of one specific process through which a certain product is being made does not entail the replicability of the same product in rather different processes and varying circumstances. For this reason, scientists and technologists rightly see the replication of a product through a substantially novel process as a proper invention, as a new technological achievement (see, e.g., Collins 1975, 210–11). Realizing a product by means of substantially novel processes counts as an independent accomplishment, which should certainly not be automatically credited to the original inventor.

Finally, the relationship between this argument against product patenting and the theory of abstraction and nonlocal meaning can be made explicit. The second type of reproducibility—the replicability of a product through unknown, potential processes—primarily involves a claim. In making this claim, scientists abstract from the processes in which the product has been realized so far, and they anticipate the possibility of novel production processes without there being any guarantee that those possibilities will be actually realizable. Hence such claims should be seen as theoretical rather than technological, as involving an extensible concept but not (yet) an invention. Put differently, such replicability claims constitute the discursive focal points for further theoretical development. They mark the start of a theoretical science that abstracts from the ways its concepts have been realized in concrete experimental or technological practices. Because theories and concepts are not patentable,[7] this argument exposes a fundamental problem of the concept and practice of product patenting.

Now it is true that to be patentable, an invention ought to be "sufficiently disclosed." In particular, the claims of the patent should be adequately supported by the description of the invention (Sterckx 2000c, 21–25). It is also the case, though, that thus far, patent offices have not taken the requirement of sufficient disclosure very seriously and have granted many extremely broad patents that lack solid support from a concrete invention. In this respect, the U.S. oncomouse patent is a typical case.[8]

In addition to these questionable practices, product patents entail a more principled problem. Once granted, a product patent confers an absolute protection on the product as such. By definition, it protects the product however it is produced or used. Because of this definition, an invention protected by a product patent can never be sufficiently disclosed, as is demanded by patent law and regulations. The fundamental problem is that sufficient disclosure of a product patent claim would require the capability to foresee all the different ways the product might be realized and used in the future. That is to say, it would require a kind of foresight or control of the future that is in principle unavailable. Conversely, granting a product patent allows its holder rights on future achievements that cannot be said to be based on the original invention. Hence granting such patents lacks any plausible justification. From a scientific and technological perspective, a product patent claim cannot be supported by the specification of (one or more) particular inventive processes. From a legal and moral perspective, the holder of a product patent is being rewarded for achievements that have not been made available. Thus this second argument undermines the very idea of product patenting.[9]

This argument differs from the usual criticisms of the patenting of inventions in the field of biotechnology and genomics. Those criticisms often employ a contrast between natural products and processes, which can be discovered, and artificial products and processes, which can be invented. The latter, but not the former, would then be patentable (see Sterckx 2000a). In contrast, my critique of product patenting distinguishes not between the artificial and the natural but rather between a concrete realization of a technological product by means of a specific process and an abstract, or conceptual, possibility of realizing this product in novel processes. Thus, although the critique applies to natural products, it does not do so exclusively. The point, then, is that the argument from the conceptual character of product patent claims can be expected to be less vulnerable to criticism than the always tricky appeal to "pure nature."[10]

How to Patent the Sun

As a third and final argument against product patenting, I would like to offer the following story. The case of the success of the Human Genome Project and of the failure of the Superconducting Super Collider plan (see Kevles 1997) confirms the intuition that biologists are better entrepreneurs than are physicists. Yet if they are willing to learn from the practice of current biotechnology, there is hope for inventive physicists. For those who want to make money, even big money, I can recommend the following approach. Get a PhD in physics and do postdoctoral research in nuclear physics. Design and realize a new type of nuclear fusion bomb, for example, through a process of fusion of atomic nuclei that has not yet been employed. Finally, apply for a product patent for the product of this bomb—to be called nuclear fusion heat—in as many countries as possible. This technological invention will be clearly novel and nonobvious, and the produced heat can be industrially exploited, for instance, for the generation of electricity.[11] Hence the chances of having the patent granted will be very good, certainly in the United States but also in Europe.

Solar heat is in fact nuclear fusion heat, and hence it is protected by our product patent. Consequently, anyone who gains an economic benefit from the heat of the sun owes a certain compensation to our physicist. Farmers who grow crops, homeowners who use a solar panel for domestic heating, swimmers who enjoy sun-heated rivers, lakes, or seas: they all have to pay up. Even if the individual amounts are modest, it is easy to see that this approach provides an entrepreneurial physicist or physics department with the definitive solution to all financial worries. Again, the crucial step in this procedure is the abstraction of the extensible concept of nuclear fusion heat from the actually realized process of invention.

But is this not pure science fiction? It certainly is not. Consider again the first stage of the proposal, the application for a product patent based on the laboratory invention of the new type of fusion bomb. At this stage, one might argue that nuclear fusion heat cannot be patented because heat is not a material thing or process. This counterargument, however, presupposes a scientifically obsolete notion of materiality. From a modern, scientific point of view, heat, light, sound, and the like are as material as the more tangible bodies, such as paper clips, aircraft engines, and aspirins.

A further objection might be that nuclear fusion heat is not a novel product. In patent law, however, the criterion of novelty applies to the invention. Thus, since our fusion bomb really embodies a new invention, there is no problem at all. After all, the same argument is routinely used by proponents of the patentability of genes. In response to the criticism that genes already exist in a natural state and hence are not new, they always retort that the patentability does not apply to the gene as such but is based on its technological isolation or production in the laboratory. In the same manner, the application for a nuclear fusion heat patent is based on the specific process through which the new type of fusion bomb has been realized in the laboratory.

Finally, one might claim at this stage that only a process, and not a product, patent should be granted to our physicist. But again, this claim can be easily rebutted. As we have just seen, in this respect the case for a product patent on nuclear fusion heat is essentially similar to the case for a product patent on genes. Since many product patents on genes have been granted to date, there is no reason at all why a patent on nuclear fusion heat should be limited to a process patent.

Thus far, in agreement with the idea of a product patent, there has been no question of other processes for the production of nuclear fusion heat. Once our patentee has obtained the patent and starts collecting fees from people who make a profit on the use of solar heat, other objections may arise. Some of those people might dispute the applicability of the patent to the case of solar heat on the grounds that their uses of sunlight are not novel. This line of argumentation, however, is not hard to defuse. After all, novelty of use has never been a necessary condition for patentability. A new, nonobvious, and useful type of washing machine can surely be patented, even if its use remains as it always was.

Others, however, might object that solar heat is a natural, and hence unpatentable, thing. But again, this objection misses the point of what a product patent is. In practice, patents on naturally occurring objects have been and are still being granted. For example, in 1986 the International Plant

Medicine Company obtained a so-called plant patent in the United States on a naturally occurring plant species of potential medical utility (see Shulman 1999, 127–49). The patent was awarded in spite of the fact that this naturally occurring plant had been used for centuries throughout the South American Amazon area. More generally, Seth Shulman concludes that "companies in the developed world hold the overwhelming majority of patents on naturally occurring ingredients from the Southern Hemisphere" (133).

Moreover, Christian Gugerell—director of the Genetic Engineering Department of the European Patent Office in Munich—sees this practice as, in principle, legitimate. As he stated explicitly in an interview (Evenblij 1998), the biotechnologist who has obtained a product patent for a plant containing gene *x* is in principle entitled to exploit all modified *and* nonmodified plants possessing this gene. The fact that the (re)production of that gene in natural plants works by means of quite different processes than is the case in the laboratory in no way detracts from the rights of the holder of this product patent. An analogous conclusion applies to the essentially similar case of nuclear fusion heat.

Before concluding, we need to consider one more move, which may be called "the ultimate objection." Opponents of patenting the heat of the sun might point out that jurisprudence allows lawyers and judges to refrain from strictly applying the explicit rules of patent law and regulations. Thus they may counter that, in real practice, the claim that solar heat is covered by the original product patent will certainly be rejected, because it is simply absurd!

With this objection I cannot but agree. Indeed, a procedure that allows an individual person or institution to exploit the full economic value of the heat of the sun for private purposes does not make sense. Hence my third argument involves a reductio ad absurdum of the concept and practice of product patenting. That is to say, it exemplifies a type of reasoning that shows the excessiveness of this activity by expounding its utmost consequences. Strictly speaking, such an argument does not imply a logical refutation. But it is eminently suitable to demonstrate that there is something badly wrong with the activity in question. After all, who wants to advocate the patentability of the sun?

The Theoretical and Moral Illegitimacy of Product Patents

What should be the conclusion of this discussion of the concept and practice of product patenting? As to the concept of product patenting, the core of my critique is contained in the second argument, which can be summarized as follows. By definition, an invention protected by a product patent can never be sufficiently disclosed, because this would require foresight about or control of all the different ways the product might be realized and used in the future. Conversely, granting a product patent allows its holder rights on unknown, future achievements that cannot be credited to the original inventor. Hence granting such a patent lacks any theoretical justification.

As to the practice of product patenting, consider the following two facts. First, it is undeniable that thus far the national patent offices, especially in the United States, have granted many very broad patents, including many product patents. Second, in several of the cases in which those patents have been litigated in court, the claims of the holders of overbroad patents have been rejected by the court. Sometimes the latter fact is used to argue that, in practice, the granting of broad and product patents is not really a problem because what counts is the result of litigation in specific infringement actions. This argument, however, is unconvincing for two important reasons. First, the manifest malfunctioning of our patent agencies has led to many protracted legal battles. These battles waste increasing amounts of time, money, and human resources. Second, it is also true that many of the granted broad and product patents are never challenged in court: for smaller firms litigation is often far too expensive, while big firms often avoid lengthy and complicated legal action through the common practice of cross-licensing.

The main moral problem of granting overbroad patents is, of course, that the patentees are rewarded for inventions that they have not really made available. In the case of product patents, this problem is intrinsically connected to the definition of those patents. To date, quite a few commentators have claimed that overbroad patents present a major problem, which may not be resolvable by ad hoc adjustments of our patenting practices

(Shulman 1999; Sterckx 2000c; Van den Belt 2002). My account of the concept and practice of product patenting supports this claim. Given our current patent laws and regulations, pure product patents should not be granted at all, while broad patents are legitimate only if the processes for which they claim protection can be shown to be plausible extrapolations of the original invention.

17

EPILOGUE: EXPERIENCE, NATURALISM, AND CRITIQUE

The principal aim of part 1 of this book is to explain and vindicate a general theory of observation, both in everyday life and in science. Observing the world requires the material realization and conceptual interpretation of observational processes. What is observable and what it is that we observe at a particular moment depend, among other things, on the available conceptual interpretations. In this sense, these conceptual interpretations can be said to structure the world. In part 2, however, I show that concepts also abstract from the world. Extensible concepts are abstract entities. They possess a nonlocal meaning that transcends the meaning they have as interpretations of established observational processes. In conceiving the world, we aim to go beyond the set of observational processes we happen to have realized thus far.

The arguments in this book follow a general strategy one often encounters in philosophical research. This strategy involves three, not necessarily successive, steps: the basic philosophical claims must be introduced and explained in a clear and coherent fashion, existing and potential criticisms of these claims need to be discussed and rebutted, and alternatives to the proposed claims should be shown to be inadequate, either for intrinsic reasons or by comparison with the claims that are being advocated. Philosophical accounts that meet these three criteria may be called plausible. In developing the account of how human beings observe and conceive the world I have adhered to this threefold strategy. In this way, I hope to demonstrate the philosophical plausibility of this account.

In this epilogue, I briefly address three more general subjects: the relationship between the proposed notion of observation and the more general, commonsense idea of human experience; the extent to which my philosophical approach may be called naturalistic; and some more general arguments for advocating the theory of abstraction and nonlocal meanings.

Observation and Commonsense Experience

In common language, the notion of experience is often used in a rather broad sense. People claim to be experienced lovers, to have had the inner experience of hearing God's voice, or to have experienced difficulties in performing an experiment or in resolving a mathematical problem. In such usages, the notion of experience primarily refers to a familiarity and skill regarding some matter of practical concern. In contrast, in many philosophical discussions—especially in epistemology and philosophy of science —experience is much more narrowly construed as sensation and more particularly as visual perception. Its philosophical significance, moreover, is mostly related to theoretical issues of justifying knowledge claims rather than to questions of practical concern.

Clearly, the broad construal of the philosophical notion of (everyday and scientific) observation developed in part 1 of this book is much closer to the commonsense usage of experience than to the conceptions of experience as a mere matter of sensation or visual perception. When we take into account the questions of how observational processes and their results are realized and interpreted in actual practice, it proves to be impossible to stick to the narrowly circumscribed views we often find in analytical epistemology. Consequently, a number of the wider commonsense connotations of the notion of experience—such as material practices and skills, learning, concept development, the sociocultural context—also play a role in the account of observation as the material realization and conceptual interpretation of scientific or ordinary observational processes.

The focus on observation, or visual experience, implies that I need to add a qualification: observation and commonsense experience are similar but they cannot be identified. As we have seen, making observations requires much more than having our eyes open. Realizing and interpreting an observational process may involve the employment of our other senses as well. The most general situation, however, is one in which the visual experience of an object is complemented by independent experiences of the same object acquired through our other senses. This clearly goes beyond the employment of hearing, touch, or smell in realizing an overall observational process for the purpose of visually perceiving the object.

Naturalistic and Antinaturalistic Characteristics

The philosophical approach practiced in this book exhibits several naturalistic characteristics. Thus my account of human observation exploits some general results from studies of vision in cognitive science. Similarly, the prime vehicle for developing my theory of abstraction and nonlocal meaning is a scientific experiment on how people may come to learn novel concepts. In addition, historical and empirical studies of the role of observation and conceptual interpretation are used throughout the book. Thus I assume that philosophy and science (the latter in the broad, European sense of the term, including the social sciences and the humanities) are not necessarily opposed to each other. More particularly, I take it to be legitimate, under certain conditions, to use robust scientific results to support philosophical arguments. However, given that scientific knowledge often changes over time and varies across paradigms and disciplines, philosophers should not use such results in an unreflective way. Even more important is to be wary of uncritically endorsing the philosophical interpretations that are claimed to be implied by those results.

In earlier work, I characterized philosophy as a theoretical, a normative, and a reflexive enterprise. In that context, the similarities and dissimilarities between the philosophical and the historical or sociological study of science are explained in detail (see Radder 1996, chap. 8). The view of philosophy as theoretical, normative, and reflexive could also provide an appropriate differentiation between philosophy on the one hand and the cognitive and natural sciences on the other. A detailed discussion of this claim, however, would go beyond the scope of the present book.

My agreement with naturalistic approaches is only partial, though. After all, some of the major claims of this book are at odds with certain doctrines that are also subsumed under the name of naturalism. This applies to the doctrine of ontological reductionism in particular. Thus, while quite a few naturalists are also ontological reductionists or even physicalists, the main trend of this book is antireductionist. For example, I explicitly argue against Paul Churchland's physicalist and reductionist interpretation of the working of connectionist networks. More generally, the account of the nature and meaning of concepts and the implied acceptance of the existence of abstract entities clearly constitutes an antireductionist and nonphysicalist position.

Taking account of both naturalistic and antinaturalistic features of observation and conceptualization is also important from a broader, social and political perspective on the role of science in society. I stress the significance of the process of material realization and the importance of the use of abstract entities (such as the nonlocal meanings of extensible concepts). Emphasizing both dimensions is especially important with respect to science. On the one hand, highlighting the material dimension of science is still needed in view of the persistence of interpretations that see science, primarily or even exclusively, as a matter of thinking, reasoning, or theorizing. On the other hand, views in which science is more or less identified with its material-productive dimension, and in which the meaning of theoretical claims is reduced to their material realizations, can also be found. The criticism of the operationalist theory of meaning, described in chapter 11, implies that such views are as one sided and hence as inadequate as the theory-dominated philosophies of science.[1]

There is also a sociopolitical side to this issue. In too many social and political debates, science is completely or primarily seen as an economic factor, as a material production force. This view wrongly neglects the relative autonomy and the specific dynamics of theoretical-conceptual work. The concept and practice of product patenting implies such a blurring of the distinction between materially realized inventions and abstract concepts or theories. Accordingly, I view the concept of product patents as philosophically unsound and the corresponding practice as legally and morally unjustified.

Beyond Ordinary-Practice Philosophy

The theory of abstraction and nonlocal meaning is an attempt to make sense of the future-oriented beliefs and actions of those involved in extending observational processes to entirely new situations. Thus this theory aims at a theoretical conceptualization of the possibility of novelty and change by means of a philosophical interpretation of the meaning of extensible concepts. In this respect, it is a forward-looking philosophical theory. This forward-looking character marks a contrast with a fairly dominant trend in contemporary philosophy. Many authors, whether or not they call themselves postmodern, are so impressed by the phenomenon of novelty and change that they declare it to be philosophically or theoretically "inconceivable."

Regarding science, this trend has its roots in the Kuhnian claim that scientific revolutions constitute radical breaks that can only be described in sociological or psychological terms. This descriptivist, backward-looking approach is characteristic of many contemporary science studies (see Nickles 1992; Radder 1996, chap. 5; 1998a; 1998b). It applies, in particular, to constructivist approaches. Here, scientific development is seen as so "contingent" that any explanation of the present, and a fortiori any extrapolation toward the future, on the basis of past developments is claimed to be futile. This view has been codified in the doctrine that nature and society are never the causes but always the results of actual constructive network interactions (see Latour 1987). In this way, change is celebrated as a brute fact, but it cannot be captured in theoretical, philosophical terms, or so it is claimed. An illustration of this is my conclusion that the theoretical concepts of actor-network theory cannot account for the future-oriented, heuristic significance of extensible concepts. In contrast, the theory of abstraction and nonlocal meaning attempts to say something philosophically relevant about the future dynamics of science, in this case about the potential extensions of concepts to possibly radically novel observational processes.

The sociology of scientific knowledge suffers from a similar lack of future orientation. In this case, the reason is the identification of the meaning of concepts with their past and present uses. Hence this approach emphasizes the structuring role of established paradigms, language games, or social goals and interests, but it does not offer any theoretical insight into how or why such frameworks might change. A typical illustration can be found in Harry Collins's Wittgensteinian account of what it means to be maximally humanlike. "It is hard to say what the essence of human-likeness is, although this is what we are groping toward. What we know is that it will have something to do with what can be learned from *socialization* and something to do with making what will be seen as *proper* responses under unanticipated circumstances" (Collins 1990, 194, emphasis added).

Again, the occurrence of change, or of unanticipated circumstances, is explicitly acknowledged. People's responses to change, however, are conceptualized on the basis of a static philosophical theory of human beings: what constitutes humanlikeness and what structures the actions of individuals is conformity to the established social context. What is clearly lacking is a philosophical account of how people may try to break away from their local social contexts. In contrast, the theory of abstraction and nonlocal meaning is an attempt at a philosophical conceptualization of our human condition that accounts for processes of change and novelty in the development of concepts.

In an interesting article, Matthew Sharpe (2002) draws attention to Herbert Marcuse's theory of universals and its employment in a critique of ordinary language philosophy. Marcuse's approach to ordinary language philosophy parallels my critique of contemporary "ordinary-practice" philosophy in two significant ways (see Marcuse 1968, chaps. 7, 8). First, he argues for the importance of a realist interpretation of universals as a vehicle for conceptualizing novelty and transcending established ways of thinking. Because there are significant differences between universals and nonlocals (as I briefly explain in chapter 11), I cannot endorse the substance of Marcuse's dialectical theory of universals. What I share, however, is Marcuse's impulse for advocating a theory of universals in the first place.

Next, Marcuse criticizes Ludwig Wittgenstein's exclusive emphasis on description of ordinary language and his corresponding rejection of theoretical explanation and critical thinking. The same emphasis can be found in the ordinary-practice philosophy that characterizes much of present-day science studies. Thus Bruno Latour (1988, 164) sharply criticizes the search for theoretical explanations of science, because what it aims for would be both unreachable and undesirable. Collins is even more explicit about his commitments when he paraphrases Wittgenstein by claiming that the sociology of scientific knowledge has no intention at all to criticize science, because at the end of the day it leaves science exactly as it found it (Collins 1996, 230). As I have argued in detail elsewhere, the consequence of such approaches is a lack of relevance regarding the future of science, both epistemically and sociopolitically.[2] In line with these arguments, the conclusion of the philosophical discussions in this book is that the study of science should go beyond the one-dimensional, backward-looking philosophies and seek to develop a forward-looking approach to the epistemic and sociopolitical problems of our technoscientific world.

Chapter 2 / The Absence of Experience in Empiricism

1. See Carnap (1966, 226). The same view is expressed in Nagel (1961, 79–81, 350).

2. To be fair, I should add that, in response to criticism, Van Fraassen has discussed the issue of observation and experience in somewhat more detail in his more recent work (see Van Fraassen 2001, 2002). Yet these studies do not confront and solve the problems stated below either.

3. For this interpretation, see Van Fraassen (1980, 1989, 2002); for some evaluations, see Hooker and Churchland (1985), Radder (1989, 300–304), Psillos (1999, chap. 9), and Muller (2005). In spite of my critical assessment of Van Fraassen's account of observation and observability, I am quite sympathetic to some other parts of his general interpretation of science. In particular, I should mention his pragmatic approach to explanation (see Van Fraassen 1980, chap. 5) and his critique of scientistic metaphysics and the corresponding emphasis on the stance character of philosophical views (see Van Fraassen 2002).

4. Fred Muller has attempted to fill out this lacuna for the notion of observability. In fully naturalistic fashion, he proposes a scientific criterion and definition of this notion in terms of the physical interactions between the object, the light, and the eye (2005, 81–83). However, as I have pointed out elsewhere (Radder 1989, 303), a fundamental problem of such scientific accounts of observability is that the relevant theories refer to unobservable entities (most obviously in the case of light). Consequently, given Van Fraassen's distinction between epistemic belief and pragmatic acceptance, consistent constructive empiricists lack any ground for belief in the truth of these theories. Thus they cannot believe Muller's account of observability either.

5. Let me note here in passing that this argument slips from "observing something is not theory dependent" to "the observability of something is not theory dependent."

6. This problem might undermine a fundamental pillar of Van Fraassen's entire philosophy of science. After all, it seems quite likely that the question of which types and practices of observation are relevant can only be answered in a context-dependent way. If this is the case, empirical adequacy proves to be a relation not just between theory and experience but between theory, experience, and their context. Hence, in analogy to Van Fraassen's own argumentation regarding the issue of explanation (1980, 156), the conclusion that empirical adequacy is not an epistemic but rather a pragmatic notion might be difficult to avoid.

Chapter 3 / The Conceptual Analysis of Observation

1. For example, I hardly deal with the much-discussed question of whether or not Hanson's views lead to (some form of) relativism or subjectivism. For some analyses of the wider philosophical implications of Hanson's notion of theory ladenness, see Suppe (1977, 151–57, 192–99), Derksen (1980, 235–61), and Adam (2002, 51–98).

2. The reason is that the typical observations of ordinary life and scientific practice relate events in a causal way. Sense-datum observations, in contrast, exclude any reference to causal relations. Thus Hanson shares the Kantian view that causality is imposed by our theories on our observations (1972, 58–65). This connection between theory ladenness and "causality ladenness" is emphasized in Heidelberger (2003, 139–40).

3. Analogous questions about the notion of theory ladenness have been raised by Fodor (1984).

4. See also Churchland's criticism of this claim (1989, 258–59). In addition, there is some evidence contradicting Fodor's main example of the universality of the theory ladenness in the Müller-Lyer illusion. Some peoples, for instance the South African Zulus, hardly seem to experience this illusion (see the discussion in Heelan 1983, 83–86).

5. The problem is that Hanson takes the results of psychological experiments too much at face value. He unreflectively translates experimental claims about perception, which are obtained under artificially realized conditions, to claims about perception in ordinary life and scientific practice. In line with the recent literature on experimentation, however, it is important to bear in mind that the results of (psychological) experiments cannot simply be extrapolated to conditions that differ significantly from the original laboratory conditions (see, e.g., Radder 1996, especially chaps. 2, 4, and 6).

Chapter 4 / The Interaction-Information Theory of Observability
and Observation

1. On the basis of his comprehensive account of experimental error, Giora Hon has advocated a similar normative claim (see Hon 2003). Kosso's case studies show, however, that it cannot be taken for granted that scientific observations or experiments will always, or even mostly, conform to this norm.

2. In a similar vein, Matthias Adam argues that, in general, the epistemic value of theory-dependent tests has nothing to do with the independence of interpretation but is rather based on the empirical nature and reliability of the relevant observations (see Adam 2004).

Chapter 5 / Connectionist Accounts of Observation

1. For more general accounts and evaluations of connectionism than are given here, see Churchland (1989, part 2; 1992a), Bechtel and Abrahamsen (1991), Dreyfus (1992, xxxiii–xxxix), Best (1992, 258–84), Meijering (1993), and Horgan (1997).

2. For the symbol manipulation approach to artificial intelligence, see also chapter 12.

3. Thus the successful operation of such a network does depend on rules. To be sure, there is also a mode of learning, called unsupervised learning, in which no desired output vectors are specified in advance. Yet in all connectionist networks, rules have been built in, namely, the rules that bring about the specific vector-to-vector transformations in activation space. These rules differ from the logical rules of symbol manipulation, but they are explicitly identifiable rules nonetheless. They may not be transparent to the average user of the network, but the same applies to the average user of a complicated symbol manipulation program (compare with Horgan's illuminating 1997 analysis of nonsentential computationalism and its relationship to classical approaches in cognitive science).

4. Note also that, in this experimental setting, we are dealing with artificial mines and rocks. As far as I know, the network under discussion has not been tested on real mines and real rocks, which may, for example, be slightly covered with plants.

5. Compare with Collins (1990). See also the various contributions to the Symposium on "computer discovery and the sociology of scientific knowledge" (1989), in particular, Brannigan (1989).

6. For the case of the intentionality of human observation, this argument empha-sizes the difference between exhibiting intentionality (which is a feature of individ-ual observers) and explaining intentionality (which requires reference to a broader observational process).

7. In Radder (1988), I argue more generally for the significance of conceptual-theo-retical work (next to experimental and formal-mathematical activity) as a separate dimension of scientific practice.

8. See the quotations at the beginning of this section. In contrast, Bechtel and Abrahamsen's views of what connectionist networks can, and cannot, achieve seem to be compatible with the account put forward here. "Our experience does not consist simply in processing discrete pieces of information. We live in a body, interact with an environment, and play roles in various social structures. . . . This may mean that networks cannot completely share our sense of similarity and gen-eralize as we do unless they share these other features of human existence as well" (1991, 122).

Chapter 6 / A Hermeneutical Approach to Perception

1. Similar claims on the directness of the observation of "theoretical" entities have been made by various other authors. See, for example, Shapere (1982), Hacking (1983, 181–85), and Pacherie (1995, 183–85).

2. For the contrast with the older Diltheyan notion of a hermeneutical circle, see Rouse (1987, 181–83).

3. In a similar sense, Davis Baird emphasizes the significance of a scientific herme-neutics of material representation, as distinct from a textual hermeneutics (2003, 52).

4. In a similar spirit, David Gooding (2003) argues for the anthropological and so-ciocultural priority of visual, qualitative, and analogue representations over verbal, quantitative, and digital representations of the world.

5. For discussions of other aspects of Heelan's philosophy of science, see Fuller (1988, 122–27), Ihde (1991, part 2), and, in particular, Babich (2002), a collection of essays in honor of Heelan.

6. For my own views on existence claims of, among other things, phlogiston, see Radder (1988, chap. 4).

7. See also Jürgen Habermas's views on the interdependence of experience and instrumental action (1978, chaps. 5 and 6); for a review and discussion, see Radder (1988, chaps. 1 and 2).

8. To avoid misunderstanding, it should be stressed that these arguments are not meant to imply that, after all, objective space is Euclidean. Within the context of developing an adequate account of experience, I merely point out the implied tension between the method of profile variation and the theory of hyperbolic vision. One might add (as an irony of history) that, according to many, the strongest arguments for the non-Euclidean character of space derive from the theory of general relativity, which happens to be one of the most abstract results of the scientific approach to nature.

Chapter 7 / The Material Realization and Conceptual Interpretation
of Observational Processes

1. Obviously, my characterization of this view as a "fallacy" implies that I do not agree with it. The issues at stake are rather complex, though, and they require a detailed and differentiated discussion. In the second part of this book, in particular in chapters 8–11, I provide such a discussion.

2. In earlier work (Radder 1988, chap. 3; see also Radder 1996, chap. 2), I used the notion of material realization in a more specific way. For the purpose of addressing epistemological questions of experimental science (in particular, the question of scientific realism), I introduced a specific procedure for obtaining a description of the material realization of a particular experiment, in contrast to its theoretical description. In the present context, I employ the notion of material realization in its most general sense.

3. In addition to the works cited above, see Hurley (2001), for an approach oriented toward the psychology of perception; Gooding (1990), for an account inspired by the history of science; and Lelas (2000), for a naturalistic philosophical interpretation that builds primarily on evolutionary biology and the neurosciences.

4. See also Heelan (1983, 151–53), Derksen (1980, 248–50), and Churchland (1989, 262–63).

5. I do not scrutinize here the philosophical ramifications of the conceptual relativism that is implied in these claims. For an analysis of the significance of conceptual relativism for the problem of scientific realism, see Radder (1988, chap. 4).

6. With respect to science, it is especially David Gooding who stresses this point (see Gooding 1990, chap. 3). At a more general level, Srđan Lelas argues for the cognitive indispensability of an adequate sociocultural environment on the basis of the fact that, at birth, humans are "prematurely born, retarded and unspecialized mammals" (Lelas 2000, chaps. 7–8).

7. Both Hudson and Van Woudenberg support their claim that direct, unmediated perception is possible through references to the views of Dretske. But remarkably enough, whatever his earlier views, Dretske (1993, 268–69) seems to allow for the fact that observation may always be interpreted by some universally applying concept, even if he immediately dismisses this concept as uninteresting and not relevant for the further purposes of his paper.

8. See, for instance, Piaget (1972) and, in particular, the more recent studies by Baillargeon (1995) and by Spelke, Vishton, and Von Hofsten (1995).

9. Exceptions are some aspects of step 1 and, possibly, step 2. These aspects constitute conditions of the above type C.

10. For the distinction between primary and secondary instruments, see Harré (2003).

11. This does not, of course, exclude that, for epistemological purposes, it may be useful to distinguish further types and uses of instruments (see, for instance, Shapere 1982; Hacking 1983, chaps. 10–11; see also Kosso's approach, discussed in chapter 4).

Chapter 8 / How Concepts Structure the World

1. Thus Koningsveld's approach is congenial to Mary Hesse's network model of concepts (1974). This model has been adapted within the "sociology of scientific knowledge" and developed into a finitist theory of meaning (see Barnes 1983; Barnes, Bloor, and Henry 1996). In chapter 15, I discuss this theory in detail.

2. See Koningsveld (1976, chap. 5). His 1973 English book contains an analogous example.

Chapter 9 / The Extensibility of Concepts to Novel Observational Processes

1. This and the next two chapters develop the notion of abstraction introduced in Radder (1992, 1993).

2. As I explain in chapter 7, the material realization of an observational process can only be analytically distinguished from its conceptual interpretation. Moreover, a descriptive account of a particular material realization necessarily involves the use of certain concepts, and thus this account should not be confused with the process of material realization itself.

3. In Radder (1996) I develop the notion of nonlocality in two different ways by distinguishing between nonlocal patterns (in the development of science and technology) and nonlocal meanings (of reproducible experiments). Here I exclusively address the issue of the nonlocality of meaning.

The term "nonlocality" is also employed in (philosophical interpretations of) quantum theory. In this context, it means that a specific type of action at a distance may occur between objects that do not interact through ordinary causal processes in space and time (see, for instance, d'Espagnat 1976). Although my use of the term nonlocal is not derived from the quantum-theoretical notion, there is one (admittedly, rather general) parallel. Just as nonlocal quantum interactions cannot be identified with the sum of a fixed number of local, causal interactions, so nonlocal meanings cannot be identified with the sum of the meanings of a determinate set of local realizations.

4. Substantiating this view would go far beyond the scope of this book, but the following points suggest some of the possible arguments: the mental representation account faces problems in view of the intersubjective character of the meaning of concepts; the definition account is deficient because it is limited to the realm of language and thus has no clue of what concepts are about; the realist view presupposes an implausible metaphysics of a ready-made world and hence it cannot account for the creative, structuring function of concepts.

5. In a somewhat different context, Thomas Kuhn points out the inappropriateness of aiming at a full definition of concepts, which would fix its applicability to every conceivable object. He comments that "this incompleteness of definitions is often called 'open texture' or 'vagueness of meaning,' but those phrases seem definitely askew. Perhaps the definitions are incomplete, but nothing is wrong with the meanings. That is the way meanings behave!" (1970a, 19).

6. See Kripke (1972), Putnam (1975), Visser (1991), and Stokhof (2000, chap. 4). For a detailed, critical evaluation of this theory, see Radder (1988, chap. 4).

7. Note the important contrast with the view that the meaning of a concept is given by its definition, whereas its relation to the world is a matter of "mere application."

Chapter 10 / Extensible Concepts, Abstraction, and Nonlocals

1. On this subject, see also the assessment of the operationalist theory of meaning at the end of chapter 11.

2. Note also that, although summarizing does involve leaving out and setting apart, the reverse is not true. Hence the proposed notion of abstraction does not (necessarily) entail the idea of summarizing.

3. Thus this view is a specific version of a nonactualist, realist ontology. Compare with Bhaskar (1978) and Harré (1986).

4. See Radder (1996, 11–26). Note that there are some similarities between replicable experimental results and what Bogen and Woodward (1988) call phenomena. But there are also dissimilarities: see the comments on Bogen and Woodward's philosophical interpretation of phenomena in Radder (1996, 36–38).

5. For a more detailed account of this case, see Pickering (1995b, chap. 3).

6. Contrary to Rainer Lange's suggestion (1999, 31, 75–77), my account of the abstraction of replicable experimental results is not similar to Paul Lorenzen's abstraction procedure, since the latter shares some crucial assumptions with the classical doctrine of abstraction. Let me add, in parentheses, that what does seem to be right is Lange's claim that my account of the coreference relation between conceptually discontinuous, theoretical terms exemplifies an operational equivalence relation in the sense of Lorenzen's theory of abstraction (see Lange 1999, 30, and compare Radder 1988, chaps. 4, 5).

7. The present definition of the referent of a replicable result, the nonlocal, is preferable to the one I gave in Radder (1996, 82–85).

8. Some recent studies of animal behavior ascribe the capacity to have concepts to certain primates, but the issue remains quite controversial (Stephan 1999; see also the brief discussion of this subject in chapter 7 above).

9. See Lowe (1995, 513–18). Lowe also distinguishes a third, a Fregean, conception of abstractness. Since this conception is not relevant to my discussion, I leave it aside.

10. I think that neither human-independent potentialities nor their contingent realizations are abstract entities. However, since my primary subject is extensible concepts and their referents, arguing for this claim here—especially the potentialities part—would distract too much from my main line of argumentation. For a cri-

tique of Platonist interpretations of laws of nature and a defense of an Aristotelian account of laws as potentialities, see Sfendoni-Mentzou (1994).

11. The (anti-Platonist) ontological claim that there are no "isolated" nonlocals parallels the epistemological position of referential realism (see Radder 1988, chaps. 4 and 5; Radder 1996, chap. 4). According to this kind of realism, we know that a descriptive term occurring in a statement of an experimental result refers to an element of a human-independent reality, if the material realization of the process from which the result results is reproducible. Thus, in this view, fixing the reference of a single term depends on the realizability of the entire experimental process.

12. For other, nonphysicalist accounts of emergence, see Bhaskar (1979, 124–37), Humphreys (1997), and Emmeche, Køppe, and Stjernfelt (1997).

13. Thus, in this conception, perceptual and hermeneutic processes display some important similarities (in contrast to Ihde 1990, 80–97). This argument exploits an account of observation for the purpose of illuminating the process of reading. As we have seen, Patrick Heelan's approach takes the reverse route: he starts from a hermeneutical interpretation of reading a written text and then extends this interpretation to the perception, or "reading," of the result, or "text," of a measuring operation.

14. To be more precise, I should of course speak here of the abstracting component of the meaning of "extensible concept." However, except where it leads to misunderstanding, I omit this qualification since its consistent usage would produce unnecessarily awkward phrases.

Chapter 11 / Wider Philosophical Implications

1. Of course, there may be other sources of linguistic ambiguity, such as the metaphorical or poetic usages of language.

2. For space perception, see, for example, Heelan (1983); for color, see, for example, Van Brakel (1993).

3. This response is also partially different from my assessment of operationalism in Radder (2002, 610–12).

4. See, for instance, Nowak (1980) and Giere (1988, chap. 3); for a more differentiated account, which also emphasizes the differences between abstraction and idealization, see Rol (2005).

Chapter 12 / Abstraction, Formalization, and Digitization

1. Note the connection between formal systems and abstraction. In a similar vein, Peter Slezak claims that certain artificial intelligence programs are capable of making autonomous scientific discoveries, and he considers this to be a test, and refutation, of the sociology of scientific knowledge. He also emphasizes the abstract nature of artificial intelligence. "Just as Turing was concerned to abstract human intelligence from its inextricable embodiment in a 'context' of other human bodily qualities, so our own test is designed to abstract science from its contingent embodiment in a ubiquitous social context" (1989, 566). For some replies from proponents of the sociology of scientific knowledge, see Brannigan (1989) and Collins (1989).

2. See Radder (1996, 180-83) for an account and critique of these transformations in the case of computer chess.

3. In addition, it is questionable whether the alphabet is really digital and whether the meaning of a poem is always unaffected by its graphical representation (compare with Collins 1990, 26-28). The roman a and the italicized *a* are clearly instances of the same letter. Yet italicizing words differently may change the meaning of a sentence. Just think of the following three questions (discussed by Van Fraassen [1980, 127] in a rather different context): Why did *Adam* eat the apple? Why did Adam *eat* the apple? Why did Adam eat the *apple*?

Chapter 13 / Aristotelian Abstraction and Scientific Theorizing

1. See also Cartwright (1999, 71-72). Joseph Rouse (1987, 9-12) includes her in a group of philosophers he calls the new empiricists.

2. Cartwright's work—in particular her more recent endorsement of Aristotelian natures, her inclusion of tendencies, and her account of the epistemic role played by scientific experiments (see 1999, chap. 4)—shares a number of important insights with Roy Bhaskar's philosophical interpretation of science (1978; compare with Gibson 1983; Chalmers 1987).

3. Compare with my remarks at the end of chapter 11. Paul Humphreys (1995, 159), however, claims that, ultimately, Cartwright fails to sustain a clear distinction between abstraction and idealization.

4. For a thoughtful analysis and assessment of Nowak's views, see Kirschenmann (1985, 1990).

Chapter 14 / Abstraction and the Extension of Actor Networks

1. Initially, Latour defines the notion of translation as the reinterpretation and displacement of "interests." Later on in his 1987 book, he uses it as applying to elements of networks and results of network interactions in general. For a more extensive review of Latour's theory, including its contrast to the sociology of scientific knowledge, see Sismondo (1996, 113–26).

2. In doing so, I develop an argument first sketched in Radder (1993, 344).

3. Similar views have been expressed by Joseph Rouse (1987, 111–19) and Nancy Cartwright. The latter, for instance, claims that physicists "do not take the laws they have established in the laboratory and try to apply them outside. Rather, they take the whole laboratory outside, in miniature. . . . The conclusion I am inclined to draw from this is that, for the most part, the laws of physics are true only of what we make" (1999, 46–47).

4. See Collins's (1985) discussion of why, in scientific practice, experimental replications are often preferred over "exact" reproductions.

5. A similar conclusion applies to Rouse's view, as expressed in the following quotation. "The claim is not that scientific knowledge has no universality, but rather that what universality it has is an achievement always rooted in local know-how within the specially constructed laboratory setting. The empirical character of scientific knowledge is the result of an irreducibly local construction of empirical reference rather than the discovery of abstract, universal laws that can be instantiated in any local situation" (1987, 119). It has been a major aim of the theory of nonlocal meaning to provide an alternative to both claims put forward in the last sentence of this quotation.

6. For some further discussion of such a science-as-technology view, see Radder (2003b).

7. I confine myself here to the basic issue. For a more detailed assessment of Latour's account of scientific laws and theories, see Kreiter (1999).

8. In Radder (1998a, 1998b), I point out the political drawbacks of the actor-network theory, which are also due to its lack of a future-directed orientation. In chapter 17, I return briefly to this issue.

Chapter 15 / Meaning Finitism and the Sociology of Scientific Knowledge

1. For some more general discussions of this approach to the sociology of scientific knowledge, see Woolgar (1981), Lynch (1992), and Mermin (1998a; 1998b).

2. How much further this agreement extends will depend on how much sociology Koningsveld is willing to take on board. I think that he will not be prepared to go all the way with the sociologists (compare with Koningsveld 1973, 19–29; 1976, 139–54). Because it is not central to the aims of this chapter, I leave the issue aside.

3. See Barnes, Bloor, and Henry (1996, 119). Note that this is a specific type of naturalism. The methodological leveling does not result from the social sciences trying to imitate the natural sciences but from a sociological reconceptualization showing that the latter sciences are far more social and far less rational than is often assumed. For a more elaborate, philosophical version of this argument against methodological dualism, see Rouse (1987, chap. 6).

4. A similar tension between a historical or empirical approach, on the one hand, and the philosophical claims that are allegedly based on it, on the other, can be found more often in recent science and technology studies. Being aware of this tension is especially important when we reflect on the issue of the (potential) normative relevance of an empirical philosophy of science and technology. See Radder (1996, 112–15; 1998a; 1998b).

5. The alternative is to ignore the problem by unreflexively using interests and goals as if they are unproblematic, directly accessible data. Steve Woolgar (1981) has criticized Barnes's earlier work for this lack of reflexivity. His criticism still applies in the case of *Scientific knowledge*. Indeed, in spite of the fact that the issue of reflexivity is brought up, it is not systematically taken into account at all (as is admitted by the authors [Barnes, Bloor, and Henry 1996, xii]). For my own view of how to deal with the problem of reflexivity, see Radder (1996, chaps. 5 and 8).

6. Hence this account might be used to address David Mermin's complaint that sociological meaning finitism fails for the case of discrete concepts (see Mermin 1998a, 1998b; Bloor 1998; Barnes 1998).

Chapter 16 / Product Patenting as the Exploitation of Abstract Possibilities

1. Etzkowitz and Webster (1995, 483–84). For a more general discussion and assessment of the commercialization of university science and the private ownership of its intellectual property, see Bok (2003), Fuller (2000a), and Krimsky (2003).

2. This is the United States' phrasing of the criteria. In the European Union, the second criterion says that the technology must involve a "genuine inventive step" and the third that it must be "industrially applicable."

3. Shulman (1999, 59–60) discusses a software patent containing no less than 41 separate claims.

4. See, for the case of the oncomouse, Sterckx (2000c, 21–25). A recent study of seventy-four patents involving 1,167 claims concludes that "many patents claimed far more than what the inventor actually discovered" (Paradise, Andrews, and Holbrook 2005, 1566). A detailed discussion, and many examples, of broad patents can be found in Bostyn (2001). Bostyn also provides three reasons why the issue of broad patents is especially significant for biotechnological inventions (147–48). First, establishing the scope of an invention may be especially problematic in the case of living material. Second, since biotechnology is a rather young and developing science, it is not always easy to disclose an invention in sufficient detail. Third, in biotechnology, inventions are often characterized by their functions, and the use of functional terminology tends to broaden the scope of the claimed inventions.

5. See Shulman (1999), Sterckx (2000c, 14–15, 21–25), Bostyn (2001), and Van den Belt and Van Reekum (2002).

6. See Van Overwalle (2000, 203–4) and Bostyn (2001, 200–209). Because the know-how implied in processes of invention is often left out of their written specification, however, such reproductions may not be as easily realizable as patent regulations seem to assume (compare with Collins 1985).

7. Sterckx (2000c, 19–20). At most, the texts describing these theoretical and conceptual possibilities might be subject to copyright protection, which is a less powerful type of intellectual property protection.

8. Shulman (1999) and Bostyn (2001) have documented many other cases. Bostyn, who is not against broad and product patents as such, argues for a stricter application of the sufficient disclosure rule to prevent unduly broad claims.

9. Note that the specific arguments of this chapter do not apply to the patenting of a product exclusively on the basis of the process specified by the inventor. To be sure, there are broader criticisms of the patent system that do apply to this type of patenting. A few of the issues are briefly mentioned in the previous sections, but here I will leave these broader issues aside.

10. Compare with Jozef Keulartz's critique of the questionable uses of the notion of nature in radical ecology (1998). For a more differentiated account of nature as a metaphor, see Roothaan (2005).

11. The example is not fully fictitious. In the 1950s and early 1960s—an era when many other grandiose scientific projects were envisioned (see Kwa 1994)—producing heat through explosions of fusion bombs was considered a serious option. "On a very large scale, it is possible to use the catastrophic process [of nuclear fusion] in a semi-controlled manner, and this possibility has been seriously looked into. A large canyon could be lined with concrete and fitted with a concrete roof so as to produce a giant steam boiler. Once every hour or so, a hydrogen bomb could be detonated inside the boiler so as to produce enough steam for an hour's consumption" (Enge 1969, 454).

Chapter 17 / Epilogue: Experience, Naturalism, and Critique

1. In Radder (2003b, 153–60), I discuss this subject in more detail.

2. See Radder (1996, chap. 5; 1998a; 1998b). Although writing from a different philosophical perspective, this assessment is shared by Steve Fuller when he criticizes the "ritualized political impotence of science studies" as a consequence of their "Kuhnification" (2000b, chap. 7).

REFERENCES

Adam, M. 2002. *Theoriebeladenheid und Objektivität*. Frankfurt, Germany: Dr. Hänsel-Hohenhausen.

———. 2004. Why worry about theory-dependence? Circularity, minimal empiricality and reliability. *International Studies in the Philosophy of Science* 18:117–32.

Amsterdamska, O. 1990. Surely you are joking, Monsieur Latour! *Science, Technology and Human Values* 15:495–504.

Anderson, M. L. 2003. Embodied cognition: A field guide. *Artificial Intelligence* 149:91–130.

Babich, B. E., ed. 2002. *Hermeneutic philosophy of science, Van Gogh's eyes, and God*. Dordrecht, Netherlands: Kluwer.

Bailer-Jones, D. Forthcoming. Standing up against tradition: Models and theories in Nancy Cartwright's Philosophy of Science. In *Nancy Cartwright's philosophy of science*, ed. L. Bovens and S. Hartmann. London: Routledge.

Baillargeon, R. 1995. Physical reasoning in infancy. In *The cognitive neurosciences*, ed. M. S. Gazzaniga, 181–204. Cambridge, MA: MIT Press.

Baird, D. 2003. Thing knowledge: Outline of a materialist theory of knowledge. In Radder 2003a, 39–67.

Barnes, B. 1983. On the conventional character of knowledge and cognition. In *Science Observed*, ed. K. D. Knorr-Cetina and M. Mulkay, 19–51. London: Sage.

———. 1998. Oversimplification and the desire for truth: Response to Mermin. *Social Studies of Science* 28:636–40.

Barnes, B., D. Bloor, and J. Henry. 1996. *Scientific knowledge: A sociological analysis*. London: Athlone.

Bechtel, W., and A. Abrahamsen. 1991. *Connectionism and the mind*. Oxford, UK: Blackwell.

Berns, E. 1979. Jacques Derrida en de taalfilosofie. In *Denken in Parijs*, ed. E. Berns, S. IJsseling, and P. Moyaert, 141–69. Alphen aan de Rijn, Netherlands: Samson.

Best, J. B. 1992. *Cognitive psychology*. St. Paul, MN: West Publishing Company.

Bhaskar, R. 1978. *A realist theory of science*. Hassocks, UK: Harvester Press.

———. 1979. *The possibility of naturalism*. Brighton, UK: Harvester Press.

Biesta, G. 1992. *John Dewey: Theorie en praktijk.* Delft, Netherlands: Eburon.

Bijker, W. E., T. P. Hughes, and T. Pinch, eds. 1987. *The social construction of technological systems.* Cambridge, MA: MIT Press.

Blokhuis, P. 1985. *Kennis en abstraktie.* Amsterdam: VU Uitgeverij.

Bloor, D. 1992. Left and right Wittgensteinians. In Pickering 1992, 266–82.

———. 1996. Idealism and the sociology of knowledge. *Social Studies of Science* 26:839–56.

———. 1998. Changing axes: Response to Mermin. *Social Studies of Science* 28: 624–35.

Bogen, J., and J. Woodward. 1988. Saving the phenomena. *Philosophical Review* 97: 303–52.

Bok, D. 2003. *Universities in the marketplace: The commercialization of higher education.* Princeton, NJ: Princeton University Press.

Bostyn, S. J. R. 2001. *Enabling biotechnological inventions in Europe and the United States.* Munich, Germany: European Patent Office.

Brannigan, A. 1989. Artificial intelligence and the attributional model of scientific discovery. *Social Studies of Science* 19:601–13.

Bridgman, P. W. 1961. *The logic of modern physics.* New York: Macmillan.

Carnap, R. 1952. Empiricism, semantics, and ontology. In *Semantics and the philosophy of language,* ed. L. Linsky, 208–28. Urbana: University of Illinois Press.

———. 1966. *Philosophical foundations of physics.* New York: Basic Books.

Cartwright, N. 1983. *How the laws of physics lie.* Oxford, UK: Clarendon.

———. 1989. *Nature's capacities and their measurement.* Oxford, UK: Clarendon.

———. 1999. *The dappled world.* Cambridge: Cambridge University Press.

Chalmers, A. 1987. Bhaskar, Cartwright and realism in physics. *Methodology and Science* 20:77–96.

Churchland, P. M. 1989. *A neurocomputational perspective: The nature of mind and the structure of science.* Cambridge, MA: MIT Press.

———. 1992a. A deeper unity: Some Feyerabendian themes in neurocomputational form. In Giere 1992, 341–63.

———. 1992b. Reconceiving cognition. In Giere 1992, 475–80.

Collins, H. M. 1975. The seven sexes: A study in the sociology of a phenomenon, or the replication of experiments in physics. *Sociology* 9:205–24.

———. 1985. *Changing order: Replication and induction in scientific practice.* London: Sage.

———. 1989. Computers and the sociology of scientific knowledge. *Social Studies of Science* 19:613–24.

——. 1990. *Artificial experts: Social knowledge and intelligent machines.* Cambridge, MA: MIT Press.

——. 1996. In praise of futile gestures: How scientific is the sociology of scientific knowledge? *Social Studies of Science* 26:229–44.

Collins, H. M., and S. Yearley. 1992. Epistemological chicken. In Pickering 1992, 301–26.

Derksen, A. A. 1980. *Rationaliteit en wetenschap.* Assen, Netherlands: Van Gorcum.

De Ruiter, W. 1992. *De evolutie van de laser.* PhD diss., Eindhoven University of Technology, Netherlands.

d'Espagnat, B. 1976. *Conceptual foundations of quantum mechanics.* 2nd ed. London: W. A. Benjamin.

Dretske, F. 1981. *Knowledge and the flow of information.* Cambridge, MA: MIT Press.

——. 1993. Conscious experience. *Mind* 102:263–83.

Dreyfus, H. L. 1992. *What computers* still *can't do.* Cambridge, MA: MIT Press.

Emmeche, C., S. Køppe, and F. Stjernfelt. 1997. Explaining emergence: Towards an ontology of levels. *Journal for General Philosophy of Science* 28:83–119.

Enge, H. A. 1969. *Introduction to nuclear physics.* Reading, MA: Addison-Wesley.

Etzkowitz, H., and A. Webster. 1995. Science as intellectual property. In *Handbook of science and technology studies,* ed. S. Jasanoff, G. E. Markle, J. C. Petersen, and T. Pinch, 480–505. Thousand Oaks, CA: Sage.

Evenblij, M. 1998. Patent op leven. *De Volkskrant 77* (May 9): 1W.

Feyerabend, P. K. 1965. Problems of empiricism. In *Beyond the edge of certainty,* ed. R. G. Colodny, 145–260. Lanham, MD: University Press of America.

——. 1999. *Conquest of abundance: A tale of abstraction versus the richness of being.* Chicago: University of Chicago Press.

Fodor, J. 1984. Observation reconsidered. *Philosophy of Science* 51:23–43.

Fodor, J., and E. Lepore. 1996. Paul Churchland and state space semantics. In *The Churchlands and their critics,* ed. R. N. McCauley, 145–62. Cambridge, MA: Blackwell.

Franklin, J. 1994. The formal sciences discover the philosophers' stone. *Studies in History and Philosophy of Science* 25:513–33.

Fuller, S. 1988. *Social epistemology.* Bloomington: Indiana University Press.

——. 2000a. *The governance of science.* Buckingham, UK: Open University Press.

——. 2000b. *Thomas Kuhn: A philosophical history for our times.* Chicago: University of Chicago Press.

Gibson, J. J. 1986. *The ecological approach to visual perception.* Hillsdale, NJ: Lawrence Erlbaum.

Gibson, Q. 1983. Tendencies. *Philosophy of Science* 50:296–308.

Giere, R. N. 1988. *Explaining science.* Chicago: University of Chicago Press.

———, ed. 1992. *Cognitive models of science.* Minneapolis: University of Minnesota Press.

Gingras, Y. 1997. The new dialectics of nature. *Social Studies of Science* 27:317–34.

Glendinning, S. 2000. Communication and writing: A public language argument. *Proceedings of the Aristotelian Society* 100:271–86.

Glymour, C. 1992. Invasion of the mind snatchers. In Giere 1992, 465–71.

Gooding, D. 1990. *Experiment and the making of meaning.* Dordrecht, Netherlands: Kluwer.

———. 2003. Varying the cognitive span: Experimentation, visualization, and computation. In Radder 2003a, 255–83.

Gorman, R. P., and J. Sejnowski. 1988. Learned classification of sonar targets using a massively parallel network. *IEEE Transactions on Acoustics, Speech, and Signal Processing* 36:1135–40.

Grandy, R. E. 1992. Information, observation, and measurement from the viewpoint of a cognitive philosophy of science. In Giere 1992, 187–206.

Gurova, L. 2003. Philosophy of science meets cognitive science: The categorization debate. In *Bulgarian studies in the philosophy of science,* ed. D. Ginev, 141–62. Dordrecht, Netherlands: Kluwer.

Habermas, J. 1978. *Knowledge and human interests.* 2nd ed. London: Heinemann.

Hacking, I. 1975. *Why does language matter to philosophy?* Cambridge: Cambridge University Press.

———. 1983. *Representing and intervening.* Cambridge: Cambridge University Press.

Hamlyn, D. W. 1970. *The theory of knowledge.* London and Basingstoke: Macmillan.

Hanson, N. R. 1969. *Perception and discovery.* San Francisco: Freeman Cooper.

———. 1972. *Patterns of discovery.* Cambridge: Cambridge University Press.

Harré, R. 1986. *Varieties of realism.* Oxford, UK: Blackwell.

———. 2003. The materiality of instruments in a metaphysics for experiments. In Radder 2003a, 19–38.

Haugeland, J. 1987. *Artificial intelligence: The very idea.* Cambridge, MA: MIT Press.

Hecht, E. 1987. *Optics.* 2nd ed. Reading, MA: Addison-Wesley.

Heelan, P.A. 1983. *Space-perception and the philosophy of science.* Berkeley: University of California Press.

———. 1989. After experiment: realism and research. *American Philosophical Quarterly* 26:297–308.

Heidelberger, M. 2003. Theory-ladenness and scientific instruments in experimentation. In Radder 2003a, 138–51.

Hempel, C. G. 1966. *Philosophy of natural science.* Englewood Cliffs, NJ: Prentice-Hall.

Hesse, M. B. 1974. *The structure of scientific inference.* London: Macmillan.

Hon, G. 2003. The idols of experiment: Transcending the "etc. list." In Radder 2003a, 174–97.

Hooker, C. A., and P. Churchland, eds. 1985. *Images of science.* Chicago: University of Chicago Press.

Horgan, T. 1997. Connectionism and the philosophical foundations of cognitive science. *Metaphilosophy* 28:1–30.

Hudson, R. G. 2000. Perceiving empirical objects directly. *Erkenntnis* 52:357–71.

Hughes, T. P. 1979. The electrification of America: The system builders. *Technology and Culture* 20:124–61.

———. 1983. *Networks of power: Electrification in Western Society, 1880–1930.* Baltimore: Johns Hopkins University Press.

Humphreys, P. 1995. Abstract and concrete. *Philosophy and Phenomenological Research* 55:157–61.

———. 1997. How properties emerge. *Philosophy of Science* 64:1–17.

Hurley, S. 2001. Perception and action: Alternative views. *Synthese* 129:3–40.

Ihde, D. 1990. *Technology and the lifeworld.* Bloomington: Indiana University Press.

———. 1991. *Instrumental realism: The interface between philosophy of science and philosophy of technology.* Bloomington: Indiana University Press.

Janich, P. 1998. Was macht experimentelle Resultate empiriehaltig? Die methodisch-kulturalistische Theorie des Experiments. In *Experimental essays—Versuche zum Experiment,* ed. M. Heidelberger and F. Steinle, 93–112. Baden-Baden, Germany: Nomos Verlagsgesellschaft.

Keulartz, J. 1998. *The struggle for nature: A critique of radical ecology.* London: Routledge.

Kevles, D. 1997. Big science and big politics in the United States: Reflections on the death of the SSC and the life of the Human Genome Project. *Historical Studies in the Physical and Biological Sciences* 27:269–99.

Kim, J. 1999. Making sense of emergence. *Philosophical Studies* 95:3–36.

Kirschenmann, P. P. 1985. Neopositivism, Marxism, and idealization: Some comments on Professor Nowak's paper. *Studies in Soviet Thought* 30:219–35.

———. 1990. Heuristical strategies: Another look at idealization and concretization.

In *Idealization I: General problems,* ed. J. Brzeziński, F. Coniglione, T. A. F. Kuipers, and L. Nowak, 227–40. Amsterdam: Rodopi.

——. 1996. Science, norms, and brains: On a cognitive approach to the paradigm of knowing. *Annals of the Japan Association for Philosophy of Science* 9:1–15.

Koningsveld, H. 1973. *Empirical laws, regularity and necessity.* Wageningen, Netherlands: Veenman.

——. 1976. *Het verschijnsel wetenschap.* Meppel, Netherlands: Boom.

Kosso, P. 1989. *Observability and observation in physical science.* Dordrecht, Netherlands: Kluwer.

Kreiter, E. 1999. *Theorie en praktijk: Bruno Latour en Joseph Rouse over de betekenis van wetenschappelijke theorieën.* Master's thesis, Faculty of Philosophy, Vrije Universiteit, Amsterdam.

Krimsky, S. 2003. *Science in the private interest.* Lanham, MD: Rowman & Littlefield.

Kripke, S. 1972. *Naming and necessity.* Oxford, UK: Blackwell.

Kroes, P. 1996. *Ideaalbeelden van wetenschap.* Amsterdam: Boom.

Kuhn, T. S. 1970a. Logic of discovery or psychology of research? In *Criticism and the growth of knowledge,* ed. I. Lakatos and A. Musgrave, 1–23. Cambridge: Cambridge University Press.

——. 1970b. *The structure of scientific revolutions.* 2nd ed. Chicago: University of Chicago Press.

Kwa, C.-L. 1994. Modelling technologies of control. *Science as Culture* 4:363–91.

Lange, R. 1999. *Experimentalwissenschaft Biologie: Methodische Grundlagen und Probleme einer technischen Wissenschaft vom Lebendigen.* Würzburg, Germany: Königshausen & Neumann.

Latour, B. 1983. Give me a laboratory and I will raise the world. In *Science observed,* ed. K. D. Knorr-Cetina and M. Mulkay, 141–70. London: Sage.

——. 1987. *Science in action.* Milton Keynes, UK: Open University Press.

——. 1988. The politics of explanation: An alternative. In *Knowledge and Reflexivity,* ed. S. Woolgar, 155–76. London: Sage.

Lelas, S. 2000. *Science and modernity: Toward an integral theory of science.* Dordrecht, Netherlands: Kluwer.

Looren de Jong, H., S. Bem, and M. Schouten. 2004. Theory in psychology: A review essay of Andre Kukla's *Methods of Psychology. Philosophical Psychology* 17:275–95.

Lowe, E. J. 1995. The metaphysics of abstract objects. *Journal of Philosophy* 92: 509–24.

Luper, S. 1999. Natural resources, gadgets and artificial life. *Environmental Values* 8:27–54.

Lynch, M. 1992. Extending Wittgenstein: The pivotal move from epistemology to the sociology of science. In Pickering 1992, 215–65.

Marcuse, H. 1968. *One dimensional man.* London: Sphere Books.

Meijering, T.C. 1993. Neuraal vernuft en gedachteloze kennis: Het moderne pleidooi voor een niet-propositioneel kennismodel. *Algemeen Nederlands Tijdschrift voor Wijsbegeerte* 85:24–48.

Meijsing, M. 1993. Connectionisme, plasticiteit en de hoop op betere tijden. *Algemeen Nederlands Tijdschrift voor Wijsbegeerte* 85:49–69.

Mermin, N. D. 1998a. Abandoning preconceptions: Reply to Bloor and Barnes. *Social Studies of Science* 28:641–47.

———. 1998b. The science of science: A physicist reads Barnes, Bloor and Henry. *Social Studies of Science* 28:603–23.

Moreland, J. P. 2001. *Universals.* Chesham, UK: Acumen.

Muller, F. A. 2005. The deep black sea: Observability and modality afloat. *British Journal for the Philosophy of Science* 56:61–99.

Nagel, E. 1961. *The structure of science.* London: Routledge and Kegan Paul.

Nagel, J. 2000. The empiricist conception of experience. *Philosophy* 75:345–76.

Nickles, T. 1989. Justification and experiment. In *The uses of experiment,* ed. D. Gooding, T. Pinch, and S. Schaffer, 299–333. Cambridge: Cambridge University Press.

———. 1992. Good science as bad history: From order of knowing to order of being. In *The social dimensions of science,* ed. E. McMullin, 85–129. Notre Dame, IN: University of Notre Dame Press.

Niiniluoto, I. 1999. Rule-following, finitism, and the law. *Associations* 3:83–90.

Noë, A. 2001. Experience and the active mind. *Synthese* 129:41–60.

Norman, A. 1998. Seeing, semantics and social epistemic practice. *Studies in History and Philosophy of Science* 29:501–13.

Nowak, L. 1980. *The structure of idealization.* Dordrecht, Netherlands: Reidel.

Olazaran, M. 1996. A sociological study of the official history of the perceptrons controversy. *Social Studies of Science* 26:611–59.

O'Regan, J. K., and A. Noë. 2001a. A sensorimotor account of vision and visual consciousness. *Behavioral and Brain Sciences* 24:939–73.

———. 2001b. What it is like to see: A sensorimotor theory of perceptual experience. *Synthese* 129:79–103.

Pacherie, E. 1995. Do we see with microscopes? *Monist* 78:171–88.

Paradise, J., L. Andrews, and T. Holbrook. 2005. Patents on human genes: An analysis of scope and claims. *Science* 307 (March 11): 1566–67.

Piaget, J. 1972. *Psychology and epistemology.* London: Penguin.

Pickering, A., ed. 1992. *Science as practice and culture.* Chicago: University of Chicago Press.

———. 1995a. Beyond constraint: The temporality of practice and the historicity of knowledge. In *Scientific practice,* ed. J. Z. Buchwald, 42–55. Chicago: University of Chicago Press.

———. 1995b. *The mangle of practice: Time, agency, and science.* Chicago: University of Chicago Press.

Pinch, T. 1985. Towards an analysis of scientific observation: The externality and evidential significance of observational reports in physics. *Social Studies of Science* 15:3–36.

Popper, K. R. 1959. *The logic of scientific discovery.* New York: Harper & Row.

———. 1972. *Objective knowledge: An evolutionary approach.* London: Oxford University Press.

Psillos, S. 1999. *Scientific realism: How science tracks truth.* London: Routledge.

Putnam, H. 1975. The meaning of "meaning." In *Mind, language and reality: Philosophical papers,* 2:215–71. Cambridge: Cambridge University Press.

Radder, H. 1988. *The material realization of science.* Assen, Netherlands: Van Gorcum. Originally published as H. Radder. 1984. *De materiële realisering van wetenschap.* Amsterdam: VU Uitgeverij.

———. 1989. Rondom realisme. *Kennis en Methode* 13:295–314.

———. 1992. Experimental reproducibility and the experimenters' regress. In *PSA 1992,* ed. D. Hull, M. Forbes, and K. Okruhlik, 1:63–73. East Lansing, MI: Philosophy of Science Association.

———. 1993. Science, realization and reality: The fundamental issues. *Studies in History and Philosophy of Science* 24:327–49.

———. 1996. *In and about the world.* Albany: State University of New York Press.

———. 1998a. The politics of STS. *Social Studies of Science* 28:325–31.

———. 1998b. Second thoughts on the politics of STS. *Social Studies of Science* 28:344–48.

———. 1999. Conceptual and connectionist analyses of observation: A critical evaluation. *Studies in History and Philosophy of Science* 30:455–77.

———. 2001. Psychology, physicalism and real physics. *Theory & Psychology* 11:775–86.

———. 2002. How concepts both structure the world and abstract from it. *Review of Metaphysics* 55:581–613.

———, ed. 2003a. *The philosophy of scientific experimentation.* Pittsburgh, PA: University of Pittsburgh Press.

———. 2003b. Technology and theory in experimental science. In Radder 2003a, 152–73.

Rey, G. 1994. Concepts. In *A companion to the philosophy of mind,* ed. S. Guttenplan, 185–93. Oxford, UK: Blackwell.

Rol, M. 2005. Abstractie in het economisch denken: Relevantie voor beleid. *Algemeen Nederlands Tijdschrift voor Wijsbegeerte* 97:224–41.

Roothaan, A. 2005. *Terugkeer van de natuur: De betekenis van natuurervaring voor een nieuwe ethiek.* Kampen, Netherlands: Uitgeverij Klement.

Rothbart, D. 2003. Designing instruments and the design of nature. In Radder 2003a, 236–54.

Rouse, J. 1987. *Knowledge and power.* Ithaca, NY: Cornell University Press.

Russell, B. 1948. *Human knowledge: Its scope and limits.* New York: Simon and Schuster.

———. 1956. *Logic and knowledge: Essays 1901-1950,* ed. R. C. Marsh. London: Allen and Unwin.

Sfendoni-Mentzou, D. 1994. Laws of nature: *Ante res* or *in rebus? International Studies in the Philosophy of Science* 8:229–42.

Shapere, D. 1982. The concept of observation in science and philosophy. *Philosophy of Science* 49:485–525.

Sharpe, M. 2002. Do universals have a reference? On the critical theory of Herbert Marcuse. *Philosophy Today* 46:193–208.

Shimony, A. 1977. Is observation theory-laden? A problem in naturalistic epistemology. In *Logic, laws, and life,* ed. R. G. Colodny, 185–208. Pittsburgh, PA: University of Pittsburgh Press.

Shulman, S. 1999. *Owning the future.* Boston: Houghton Mifflin.

Sismondo, S. 1996. *Science without myth: On constructions, reality, and social knowledge.* Albany: State University of New York Press.

Slezak, P. 1989. Scientific discovery by computer as empirical refutation of the strong programme. *Social Studies of Science* 19:563–600.

Spelke, E. S., P. Vishton, and C. von Hofsten. 1995. Object perception, object-directed action, and physical knowledge in infancy. In *The cognitive neurosciences,* ed. M. S. Gazzaniga, 165–79. Cambridge, MA: MIT Press.

Stegmüller, W. 1970. *Theorie und Erfahrung.* Berlin: Springer.

Stephan, A. 1999. Are animals capable of concepts? *Erkenntnis* 51:79–92.

Sterckx, S., ed. 2000a. *Biotechnology, patents and morality.* 2nd ed. Aldershot, UK: Ashgate.

——. 2000b. Conclusions. In Sterckx 2000a, 365–82.

——. 2000c. European patent law and biotechnological inventions. In Sterckx 2000a, 1–112.

Stokhof, M. 2000. *Taal en betekenis: Een inleiding in de taalfilosofie.* Amsterdam: Boom.

Suppe, F. 1977. The search for philosophical understanding of scientific theories. In *The structure of scientific theories,* ed. F. Suppe, 1–241. Urbana: University of Illinois Press.

Symposium on "computer discovery and the sociology of scientific knowledge." 1989. *Social Studies of Science* 19:563–695.

Tiles, M., and H. Oberdiek. 1995. *Living in a technological culture.* London: Routledge.

Toulmin, S. 1967. *The philosophy of science.* London: Hutchinson.

Van Brakel, J. 1993. The plasticity of categories: The case of colour. *British Journal for the Philosophy of Science* 44:103–35.

Van den Belt, H. 1989. Action at a distance: A. W. Hofmann and the French patent disputes about aniline red 1860–1863, or how a scientist may influence legal decisions without appearing in court. In *Expert evidence: Interpreting science in the law,* ed. R. Smith and B. Wynne, 184–209. London: Routledge.

——. 2002. Biopatenting, "green biotechnology" and the ethos of public science. Paper for the conference on *Sozialethische Aspekte der Biopatentierung.* Tübingen, Germany, October 11–12, 2002.

Van den Belt, H., and R. van Reekum. 2002. *Issues rond octrooien en genen.* www.sls.wau.nl/mi/mgs/research_programme/genomics_essay_P04.doc.

Van Eck, D., H. Looren de Jong, and M. K. D. Schouten. 2006. Evaluating new wave reductionism: The case of vision. *British Journal for the Philosophy of Science* 57:167–96.

Van Fraassen, B. C. 1980. *The scientific image.* Oxford, UK: Clarendon.

——. 1989. *Laws and symmetry.* Oxford, UK: Clarendon.

——. 1995. Against naturalized epistemology. In *On Quine,* ed. P. Leonardi and M. Santambrogio, 68–88. Cambridge: Cambridge University Press.

——. 2001. Constructive empiricism now. *Philosophical Studies* 106:151–70.

——. 2002. *The empirical stance.* New Haven, CT: Yale University Press.

Van Overwalle, G. 2000. Biotechnology patents in Europe: From law to ethics. In Sterckx 2000a, 197–206.

Van Woudenberg, R. 2000. Perceptual relativism, scepticism, and Thomas Reid. *Reid Studies* 3 (2): 65–85.

Visser, A. 1991. Slaat het allemaal nog ergens op? Beschouwingen over incommensurabiliteit, verwijzen en werkelijkheid. In *Realisme en waarheid,* ed. J. van Brakel and D. Raven, 20–40. Assen, Netherlands: Van Gorcum.

Woolgar, S. 1981. Interests and explanation in the social study of science. *Social Studies of Science* 11:365–94.

INDEX

Abrahamsen, Adele, 43–44, 45, 54, 190n8

abstract entities: extensible concepts as, 115–18; nature and existence of, 113, 115; Popperian view of, 122–25

abstraction: classical doctrine of, 110–11, 141–42; and conceptualization of novelty, 183–84; concreteness versus, 112–13, 140–44; extensibility and, 109, 115–18; formalization and, 129, 136–37; in history of philosophy, 108–9, 138; idealization versus, 128, 139–40; as leaving out, 109, 128; and meaning, 6, 99–106, 156–57; ordinary versus scientific, 112–13, 143–44; product patenting and, 172; scientific theorizing and, 138–44; as setting apart, 109–10, 128, 141; as summarizing, 110; terminology of, 107–8; theories and, 139–40, 150–53

actions: concomitant, 74; future, 75; past, 74–75. *See also* human observers

actor networks, 145–50

Agracetus, 163, 165

Anderson, Michael, 76–77

aniline reds, 155–56

animals: observation as conducted by, 85; species-specific characteristics of, as observers, 88

antinaturalism, 181–82

apodicticity: of perception, 65, 81

approximation, 128

Aquinas, Thomas, 110

Aristotle, 6, 110, 140, 142

artificial intelligence, 129–36, 196n1 (chap. 12)

Barnes, Barry, 7, 154–62, 198n3, 198n5

bear-on-a-tree example, 27–30, 86

Bechtel, William, 43–44, 45, 54, 190n8

Bedroom at Arles (Van Gogh), 67–69

Bhaskar, Roy, 196n2 (chap. 13)

Bijker, Wiebe, 166

biotechnology industry, and patenting, 163, 166, 168–69, 176, 199n4

Bloor, David, 7, 154–62, 198n3, 198n5

body: possibility and, 75; and proprioception, 71; role of, in observational process, 28–30, 60–61, 74

Bostyn, S. J. R., 199n4, 199n8

Brahe, Tycho, 20–21, 23

Bridgman, P. W., 126

broad patents, 168–70, 177–78, 199n4

Canadian Supreme Court, 170

Carnap, Rudolf, 11–12, 122

Cartwright, Nancy, 7, 138–44, 197n3

causality in science, 138–39

causal theory of meaning, 105

certainty: perceptual, 65, 81

change, conceptualization of, 183–84